Finding Fulfillment
IN THE
Spiritual Age

Finding Fulfillment
IN THE
Spiritual Age

EDITED BY

Sheri Keys & Sheldon Ginsberg

PRESENTED BY

INSTITUTE OF
ENERGY BASED HEALTH
Your Resource for Energy Medicine & Energy Healing

Finding Fulfillment in the Spiritual Age
Edited by Sheri Keys & Sheldon Ginsberg

ISBN: 978-1-939288-21-9
Library of Congress Control Number: 2013941859

http://www.energybasedhealth.com

Presented by Institute of Energy Based Health, LLC

Published as An Imprint of Wyatt-MacKenzie
www.wyattmackenzie.com

Table of Contents

Introduction

What is spirituality?

Spirituality is a belief in something bigger than ourselves.

Why is this important?

Because when life breaks down you can turn to a Higher Power and receive guidance, solace, direction, purpose, energy, growth and whatever else you may need to find your way back to truth, balance and health.

The following book contains a collection of spiritual stories that include insights, recommendations, lifestyle changes and so much more to inspire you to reach for your own inner and outer miracles.

The stories are tragic and compelling, deep and humorous. They make you think and they touch something inside of you.

In reading through the authors' trials and tribulations, each on their road to spiritual awakening, one theme resounds loudly throughout their storytelling.

Many waited until they had a physical breakdown before embracing their current peaceful lifestyle practices.

They lived a life based on working too much and ignoring the warning signs their body's inner wisdom conveyed as they continued following a path founded on (in a nutshell) the need to please others.

If we regard the number of writers in this anthology as representation of our population's mindset it becomes clear that we, as a society, have yet to harness spirituality and transformation in a way that does not, unfortunately, involve pain and suffering.

As you read each story and identify with the writer's healthy need to take care of their family and their unhealthy need to reach a certain level of success, even at the cost of their health, pay close attention for this is a lesson worth learning.

When we learn to reach higher not because we have nowhere else to go but because we decide that the goal of Oneness is more important than anything else is when our world will experience a deep change.

In the end, we are more similar to one another than different. While our competitive world makes us focus (over-focused) on what makes us different in order to establish an identity that feels safe, it is the attachment to this identity that keeps us from experiencing a bigger spiritual picture.

It is only when we are willing to surrender to Oneness and let go of the egoic need to conquer, win and prove is when our spiritual selves rise within us.

To be clear, establishing an identity is important for it is part of the maturation process. However, at a certain point, this focus must give way to a higher pursuit. Without clear supportive directives to continue maturation by fostering a desire for Oneness while retaining individuality, many will remain stuck conquering, winning and proving themselves... forever.

If one of us is stuck, we all are stuck.

Oneness is about coming together and experiencing spirituality, any form of it, with love, compassion and acceptance.

The connection to God, Spirit, Creator, The Universe, Source, Chaos, etc.... is such a deeply personal experience indeed; it is the Ultimate Personal Experience, that the only way the population of our world can come together in any kind of meaningful way is to encompass any and all belief systems.

Everyone has access to Spirit and everyone has the right to reject its presence.

For those of you that know you know Spirit exists I say do not force your knowing upon anyone else. For the deeply personal experience those who do not believe are experiencing is at odds with yours.

Let us instead honor that at the core of each person's being is a connection with All That Is.

The only way to come together is to honor each person's experience of reality. Then and only then, can the possibility of coming together and learning as One be realized.

In the end, belief or disbelief in Spirit does not matter. Somehow we got here. The name of that process is not as important as your relationship to it. Choose for yourself and explore that choice until you reach another level of awareness.

It is this reaching that we call spirituality.

Enjoy your journey.

Sheri and Sheldon

Chapter 1

Every Thought Is A Prayer

By Helen Wood

Sitting on the uncomfortable, crinkly paper of the examination table dressed in a patient gown, my doctor status immaterial to the immunologist telling me the results of my tests.

"I'm sorry to have to tell you that we've done all we can for you. I just don't think you'll ever be able to work again. I'm recommending complete, medical social security disability for life. You should take this opportunity to provide for yourself."

For a moment, reality disappeared into a blank space. I felt his words smothering me, like a heavy black cloak being thrown over me, trying to extinguish the very light of my life. My breath caught in my throat, and for a full minute, I could not breathe. Then suddenly, a violent shudder shook my entire body. Every aspect of my being screamed, *No, you're wrong!* I could not find room for his words to enter my mind, because they did not speak my truth. I knew, to the depths of my soul, that these words would send the strongest message possible to my body and then I would never heal.

How could I have possibly arrived here? My mind reeled with flashes of the previous years. I had been working as a holistic women's health specialist in academic medicine, on the fast track, with a wealth of training and credentials. At a national level, I had built a highly successful career as a medical researcher, educator, practitioner of medicine, speaker, and a published author, having written about hormonal therapy and, ironically, stress and work-life balance. I was also the medical director of a large internal medicine clinic and a women's health clinic with annual budgets of one million dollars. I was a leader in my field. But I wore a lot of "hats", which created a heavy yoke to carry, leaving me overwhelmed and exhausted.

I was also a wife and the mother of a precious young daughter. Although I lived in a beautiful house, it was a two-hour commute to and from work every day. Where did I find the time to juggle all these responsibilities? It was robbed from my sleep, which averaged 4-5 hours per night, and from any time I might have had for myself. Running became "running around", and eating became whatever I could grab whenever I had the chance.

I lived this way for years. Even when I left academic medicine for private practice to remove a few of my "hats" to create more time, especially to spend with my daughter, my practice was bursting within four months. I found myself right back in the same lifestyle.

From the outside looking in, I had a beautiful family, a gorgeous home, and financial security. Surely, this was the stuff the "good life" was made of. But inside, I felt the echo of a deep void that I could not define or seem to fill that had been there for a very long time. I seemed captive on a very fast train, one that did not allow me time to slow down long enough to consider where I was, or where I might be headed.

I had been getting infections for several years that had now become much more frequent and severe. I had ignored the signs, attributing them to stress and exposure at work. Finally, my body just ground to a halt, and I could no longer keep up with the work schedule my practice demanded. Only when I closed it, did I seek care. The diagnosis was a serious genetic immune deficiency disorder that prevented me from producing enough antibodies to fight off common infections. After about 18 months of embracing all that traditional medicine, and a number of holistic modalities, had to offer, I had improved only minimally, not enough to be able to resume work.

Now I was facing a despairing recommendation from my immunologist. Yet, in the face of all the evidence to the contrary, *I knew for sure through my own deep source of knowing*, that I unequivocally could heal and regain a life that was fully productive and fulfilling.

Listening to and trusting in my own intuition was the start of my road back. I discovered my truth residing within me, not in external facts or in someone else's opinion.

How did I find the faith in my inner knowing to serve as the beginning of this new path? I believe my intuition, when it found itself in such deep conflict with what I was being told, suddenly soared to a much higher level of awareness to act on my behalf. And for that I am eternally grateful, beyond what words can convey. This faith gave me the initial conviction and motivation to do what needed to be done. If I had not listened, the remainder of my life would have unfolded quite differently. It became the foundation of my belief in myself.

Unfortunately, I had not always possessed this luxury. Usually, my inner voice was quieter, more like a whisper, and I needed to work to listen and stay attuned. However, over time, I discovered some key ways to connect with this source on a regular basis. And, I uncovered a power within myself that I would not have imagined I possessed.

One of the hidden "gifts" of having your life grind to a halt is that you are literally forced to slow down and be still, so it becomes much more difficult to ignore this inner voice. I have observed that the soul whispers, the mind calls, and the body screams because each is a messenger, and at the same time, they are deeply interconnected. For myself and so many others, it seems we do not listen until the body screams. But now that I had actually experienced this truth as a cosmic two-by-four hit me over the head, the whisper was validated. From that point on, I sought ways to hear that whisper more clearly.

As a member of a Unity "New Thought" Church, I had embraced its teachings intellectually, but they had not translated into actual, effective practices. However, the screams drastically changed things. I made it my first priority to schedule time, every day to be still and to quiet the chatter in my mind so that I could empty it and to turn inward to create space to listen. I embraced meditation to develop my connection with my inner source of knowing, even though my first attempts lasted less than thirty seconds. Such a seemingly simple task as just being still can be so difficult. I continued to remind myself that meditation is an acquired skill and requires just as much practice as you would for a musical instrument. Once mastered, I experienced the feeling of true oneness with myself and with what I understood to be the larger me, which I knew as Spirit.

I began practicing yoga, which not only increased my body's

strength, flexibility, and balance, but also led me to a peaceful still point of centering, and a body awareness I realized I had never truly experienced before. As a physician, you learn to tune out your body… its hunger, its need for sleep, its desire for movement, and its information about what is out of balance… all to be able to respond to whatever is required of you. Reawakening those signals took time, but they had much to tell me. I used to feel such pride at being able to function in the face of illness and pain. I realized this was an act of neglect, of not loving myself enough to nurture my body in the ways it so needed and deserved.

Around this time I also happened to read the book, *Healing Letters*, by Myrtle Fillmore, the wife of Charles Fillmore who was one of the founders of the New Thought Movement in the early 1900's. Myrtle suffered from an incurable, highly resistant form of tuberculosis and was told she would not survive. In the book, she described how she cured herself through the use of visual imagery, spending hours using every sense and all the detail she could conjure. She would "see with her mind" a healing white light spreading throughout her body, being in complete and perfect health.

Every day I did the same, for hours at a time. I imagined my DNA changing shape and its vibrational frequency assuming a state of optimal vitality. We now know that the power of this method lies in the very real fact that when you visualize something with your brain, it can't tell the difference between what is "external reality" and what is "internal reality." The same firing of brain cells by both practices establishes the same pathways. And it can be effective with just 20 to 30 minutes per day.

Meditation created the stillness and connection within, yoga reestablished my bodily awareness, and visualization became a compelling way for me to engage the power of thought on my own behalf. Then, I began to pray. Not having been raised with a faith tradition, prayer had previously felt foreign to me. But now I had come to the realization that *every thought is a prayer* and that the power that lies within that prayer is the power of intention to own at a deep emotional level rather than just asking for help. So I began to pray… many times per day. Often it was for brief moments but when possible, for more prolonged periods. I wrote my intentions down, and said them aloud to tap into the full potential to shape my reality and co-create with whatever brought me into being. I learned I could co-create and manifest at a very high level.

To deepen my level of faith in the conviction of my intention, I practiced "challenging my faith." Each day, I asked for something to occur that I could not have possibly done on my own, something that required the intervention of Spirit. Inevitably, each challenge was answered and I progressively strengthened my "faith muscle." Then, I increased the difficulty of manifestation, from simple acts of finding my keys, to receiving assistance in some manner from the most obscure origins.

I participated in a three-month Unity course in gratitude and prosperity and began to write in a gratitude journal every night, expressing thanks for all things, from the greatest in scope to the smallest acts of kindness. Throughout the day, I placed my attention on noticing when anything positive occurred, and when it did, I said a small prayer of thank you, aloud if I could. I came to view gratitude as another reflection of intentional prayer. This practice kept me connected not only with each moment in which our power to manifest truly lies, but with a widely expanded perspective that shifted any temptation to narrowly magnify my own challenges to a telescopic view that could somehow see that there is a reason for everything.

Gratitude is such a profound practice. When you express appreciation for something, it's a powerful way of mirroring to the Universe exactly what you want, and your request for more of the same. This loving and intelligent Universe that created us all personally responds in kind by giving back to you what you communicated you are grateful for. Gratitude opens the door for every type of abundance, as does tithing. By tithing I don't mean charitable giving through the recognition of lack somewhere. Tithing is giving back to your source of inspiration and connection, whatever that might be – a church, an organization, a person, or anything else. So, I began tithing regularly as well. And then I was in awe of the overflowing abundance that showered me from the most unexpected places. I received a refund from previously paid taxes of $34,000, and another $14,000 in back payment from a bankrupt insurance plan that supposedly had no funds to disperse.

I found myself at a crisis point of my own making when my inner knowing screamed its truth at me. Because I hadn't listened to it until that fateful day, I experienced tremendous losses in my life. My marriage didn't survive. I had to start over financially and begin a new career. But I also received precious gifts of learning and wisdom along the path. Most importantly, profound healing was activated. Within six months of engaging in the practices I've described, I returned to work part-time and then to full-time within a year. And a great blessing of discovery was learning what I'm here to do, which further accelerated my healing when I fully stepped into it and created alignment between myself and the Universe's intentions for me.

I now live that vital, productive, and fulfilling life that I believed so deeply in, that I was told by my inner knowing was the truth for me. And now it doesn't take hours each day to remain in this space, though I do need to always be conscious of whether my practices are slipping. My passion is to do all I can to assist others, especially women, to access their deepest guidance and power for lasting change so they need not hit the wall going 60 miles per hour before they get the message that I did.

When you fully and simultaneously engage the power of your spiritual connection you are inspired through emotions and the wisdom of your body's awareness to move forward into guided action to co-create with the Universe. Then, what is possible becomes truly unlimited.

Bio

Dr. Helen Wood, The Body and Soul MD, is **multi-faceted holistic** healer, transformation catalyst, and pathfinder. After overcoming a serious health challenge that was strongly contributed to by high levels of stress, Dr. Helen dedicated herself to her own soul's true calling. She empowers other professional women and intentional seekers to move beyond overwork, overwhelm, over fatigue and wondering "what it's all for" to create a business and life that feels deeply true to them, vibrantly alive, and joyous, while usually doubling or tripling their income doing what they love. She provides her clients with the high value tools that facilitate access to their deepest wisdom and power for lasting change to create profound personal shifts that transform stress, struggle, self-doubts and self-sabotage into a new clarity, confidence, and harmonious balance, while illuminating their soul's true path.

Dr. Helen's 20 years of expertise as a leading holistic women's specialist, intuitive gifts, degree in psychology, extensive training as a True Purpose coach, and mastery of over 20 proven, step-by-step trans-formational methods create the foundation for her rare ability to comprehensively address all facets of the spectrum of personal trans-formation, healing, and life vision and purpose by offering a multidisciplinary approach that fully encompasses the mind, body, and spirit.

While spending 15 years in academic medicine, Dr. Helen served as director of large internal medicine and women's health clinics with annual budgets of one million dollars. She originated the "Journey the Seven C's to Your Soul's Path" system and the Stress-SOS™ program, and is the founder of Open the Door to More. She is the author of the forthcoming book *Success Stress-SOS™: The 5 Essential Keys For Women to Transform Frazzled and Fatigued to Focused and Fully Alive.* Dr. Helen is a nationally published author in areas that include stress, work-life balance, hormonal therapy and life purpose, a presenter, a researcher and television consultant. She has been consistently selected as One of America's Top Physicians, including in 2012. She speaks and serves clients internationally to share her passion to connect women with and fully free their authentic self to express in all aspects of their lives.

Chapter 2

Enough-ness as Spiritual Fulfillment

By Denise Hughes

Many of my clients come to me as high earners... with a feeling of "never having enough money." It does not matter how much they earn, their experience is one of lack, scarcity and seeing the glass of life as half empty.

Because I believe in the power of imagination and visioning in creating what we want in life, I ask clients to begin to create images of what "enough" looks like in their lives. When I hear, "that scares me," "I'm afraid", "I don't feel it is OK to want more," "I know what others want but I'm not connected with what I want," or this invitation brings forth great emotion" my experience knows there is often an issue at the root chakra.

The root chakra is one of the seven centers of spiritual energy in the human body according to yoga philosophy. This particular chakra is about support and represents our most basic of physical needs, that of food, clothing, shelter and other basic needs for survival. When energy is blocked in this chakra, issues of safety, trust and a denial of a basic self right *to have and to be* are present.

Blocks in this chakra are aligned with a core belief that love or a part of oneself will be rejected if "more" of any form of abundance is allowed in. Money is one form of abundance, as is relationship, living on purpose, new opportunities, health and love.

It is at this base level, at the core of our being where the spiritual energy of "not enough" lives. This energy lives in the cellular memory of the body's experiences and is expressed in the feeling of deprivation, lack, or scarcity.

How did this cellular experience come into being? Usually from early trauma, neglect or basic needs not being met early in our development. We were not nourished in ways we needed to be nourished.

Each of us has our own story around this. I certainly do. Growing up with depression-era parents hammered the "not enough" mindset into my being. I internalized this mindset and through my behavior, began re-creating this experience repeatedly in my adult life until I woke up and got conscious about what I was doing.

The stories we hold to be true about "not enough," at the cellular level, are linked to limiting beliefs at the cognitive level. Here are some examples of Root Chakra beliefs contributing to "lack."

FYI - these are not rational. They usually live in our blind-spot. This is why we may not be aware of them.

"If I have more money I won't be loved."

"My family rejects friends and people who appear to have more money than they do."

"If I earn more than my husband, he will find another partner because money means manliness to him."

"If I have more money, I will be abandoned."

"If I have more money, someone will take it away from me."

"Whatever I create will be taken from me anyway."

These internalized beliefs from long ago were handed down from others who have lovingly taken care of us for much of our lives.

Earning more money will not fix the experience of deprivation in the physical world. When more money does comes in, the power of these limiting beliefs will place a teflon coating on the newly earned money to ensure it does not remain. Why? More money will begin to create an experience of enough. The core energy in our body is telling us it is not safe to bring in more for then something bad will happen.

So our behaviors (ways of thinking, doing and feeling) find ways to keep the feeling "of being broke" alive... while keeping the experience of "more or enough" out of our orbit.

This is sometimes why people spend more than they earn. Our money choices are supporting the current wiring of "not enough." It is a reason why we spend money on season tickets for the San Francisco Giants and say we cannot afford healthcare. It is why we spend money on hobbies and entertainment while struggle to pay the rent or we spend money on beauty treatments while placing groceries on a credit card because we don't have enough available funds in our bank account. When we make money choices that keep us living in the red (a place of deficit in our bank accounts and bodies) we are re-creating the "not enough" experience that keeps us living in survival mode.

Shifting to "Enough-ness"

The question then becomes, "What is necessary in supporting the energy shift in the body from a space of "not enough," to "enough?" It is important to remember this is not a cognitive process. It is a body process. Cognitive processes are intellectual, body process are experiential.

Our body experiences life through our senses, which in turn influences our nervous system. When our nervous system interprets experiences as nourishing and life sustaining, we begin to lay down new wiring... shifting from "not enough" to "enough." When our root chakra is re-wired, money, as well as other forms of abundance show up in our physical world. The great thing is these forms have sticking power for inner work creates outer results.

Imagery

Using imagery is one method of creating the shift to "enough-ness." Why? Images are mental pictures that create a new experience in our bodies in the way of feelings. Imagery lays the ground-work for "what can be created." If we can get comfortable in our bodies with imagining what "enough" feels like, we can begin to create an experience of "enough" for ourselves in our physical world. Imagery can help us move through our fear. In the book, *The Science of Getting Rich*, author Wallace Wattles tells us, "The Creative Power within us makes us into the image of that to which we give our attention."

If we bathe ourselves in imagery that makes us feel good, then we begin to actually create chemical changes in our bodies. We move from pumping adrenaline (a survival hormone) to creating endorphins (a pleasure hormone). Imagery helps us to turn on our body's internal pharmacy of good feelings, naturally.

Financing Needs First, Wants Second

Financing our true survival needs BEFORE anything else will also calm our nerve endings and give our body the experience of safety and nurturance. We can breathe more easily when we know the mortgage is paid, money is available for food on the table, gas to keep our cars running and our health care needs are met.

Happiness studies have actually shown that once our survival needs are met, more money does not necessarily make us happier.

Energy and Body Work

Energy and bodywork is foundational work to support us in re-connecting with our core. Working with my breath in yoga has taken me to deep places and in these places I have uncovered lots of stuff getting in my own way of "receiving enough in."

As I've been able to open to more receiving in my own life, I find the quality of my breath changes. My exhale is getting as long as my inhale. I am withholding less. I find I can chant with greater volume and more depth. Constrictions are released.

Besides yoga, there are other forms of energy work. EFT (Emotional Freedom Technique) founded by Gary Craig is aimed at bringing equilibrium to energy disruptions in the body.

You can explore what energy and body work feels right for you. There are many choices available to you.

Talking to Ourselves in the Spirit of Love and Compassion

Tending to our thoughts is important (what we say when we talk to ourselves). Root chakra affirmations can be… "It is safe for me to be here," "I love the wisdom of my body and trust it," "I am learning to feel the energy of love and support in the cells of my being," "I choose relationships that give love freely," and "I am the creator of my own experience today."

Taking a Seat at the Table of Our Life

For us women, we seem to give up our seats at the table of life fairly easily in order for others to have before we have. Placing our needs and desires equal to that of others is a first step in giving us the experience of "enough."

It is in my fifth decade where I am now comfortable placing my needs and desires before that of others. I am into equal energy exchanges in all areas of my life. I no longer have the desire or bandwidth to give more than I receive today. I no longer allow my Catholic upbringing and negative emotions, like guilt, to come between me and the choices I know are best for me.

Creating enough for yourself financially may look like fully funding your retirement account over fully funding your children's education. It is great if you can do both and if not, that is OK. It is OK to allow your needs to come first. Your kids have age on their side and you do not at this juncture.

Connecting With Nature

Spending time in nature is my favorite way of creating an experience of "enough" in my body. Nature continually gives us overflowing bountiful sensory experiences and fills us up from the inside out. Beauty is everywhere. There is no experience of lack in nature. One daisy does not have 4 petals while the rest have 16 petals. For all that exists, there is fully enough with equal beauty.

For eleven years, each week, I've hiked with the same women up and down a mountain in Northern California. As we hike, we sweat. The more we sweat, the more we share our deepest heartfelt joys and sorrows with one another. We have shared many miles of conversation. This is one of the most sacred spiritual connections I have in my life. Money cannot buy this. For me, connection with our deepest selves and nature is a form of bliss.

Being Grateful For What Is

One year at my husband's Tai Chi Retreat, his teacher taught us a "kindergarten gratitude" exercise for adults. Here's how it goes: Close your hands into fists and raise them above your head. Think of things you are grateful for and as you do, release one digit for each thought of gratitude, until your hands are out-stretched in the air above your head!

That was about ten years ago and I am still doing this exercise daily. Over time, I have actually felt the change in my body's chemistry. I used to be a complainer and focus on the negative. Truly, this simple little exercise has changed my life and my body's chemistry.

What we focus on, multiples in power and effect. There is a spiritual shift happening regarding the American dream. Once, the focus used to be on "more, better and bigger." The shift now in the spiritual age, is to be thankful for what we have and to live life in this space of gratitude. Simplicity is key. This is a big spiritual shift.

Inviting Money to Stick Around in Our Orbit

Think about the sticking energy that you want to create is more similar to that of Velcro rather than the stickiness of a post-it note. Invite money to stick with you in your accounts to create a cushion to fall back on. This shifts you from "living on the edge," pumping adrenaline, to having room to breath and think about choices.

Spiritual Fulfillment

Spiritual fulfillment is an inside process. When I tune into the core of my being, I listen deeply to my body's wisdom to create experiences of "enough" in my life, I feel spiritually fulfilled. This is a sacred place and space. Money cannot buy it. We spend less when living in this space because our experience is one of fullness rather than emptiness. Spiritual fulfillment is about indulging ourselves at the soul level, the deepest level of our being. Once had and reclaimed, no one can take it away. It is my inner divine light and your inner divine light that brings peace and a sense of well-being to the core of our being.

Bio

Denise Hughes is an inspirational speaker, author, lover of nature, and a sought out Financial Consultant! She lives in Northern California with her husband and two dogs.

The Wall Street Journal, Money Magazine, Financial Advisor, and other prestigious journals seek her advice on matters of love, money and relationship. Once on the brink of divorce over money matters in her own marriage, she now consults with couples, individuals and entrepreneurs on how to make money work in life and business. Her transformation inspired her to support others in transforming their money issues.

Denise has a Master of Arts in Counseling Psychology, a Certificate in Interactive Guided Imagery and a Certificate in Financial Counseling. Her approach is integrated and holistic. When she's not working, you can find her hiking mountains in Northern California with her husband.

Chapter 3

What I Know For Sure:
7 Lessons That Can Change Your Life

By Amy Scher

My inner being must have known that chaos would be good for my soul. It must have known that a magical country full of vibrant colors and sacred cows had much to teach me. And it must have known that almost dying would be the beginning of something wonderful. In fact, I know it did.

By the time I realized I would need something drastic to save my life, every muscle, nerve and cell in my body had deteriorated to a frightening place. I had brain lesions, cardiac issues, full-blown arthritis, and pain in every inch of my being. I was only 28-years-old and had lost all but my fiery personality and self-created motto: When life kicks your ass, kick back. I couldn't imagine, at the time, how this would all turn out for the odds were stacked against me and there was no hope in sight. But then, as if the slow-motion mechanism of my life suddenly shattered, everything changed.

In my book, *This Is How I Save My Life*, I write: "It came like a far-reaching branch with a prize dangling on the end—the kind you can just barely stretch out to reach. I grabbed it using the tiny amount of strength I still had from fighting. And I promised myself I wouldn't let it go, even if it broke right there in my palm and tried to take me down with it."

After years of treacherous medical treatment for chronic Lyme disease and other manifestations of a failed immune system, I was unsuccessful at re-infusing life into my tired, pain-entrenched body. Discouraged by my doctors in California, I would be the first with my disease to undergo a controversial embryonic stem cell treatment in Delhi, India. Amidst the fear, a little whisper inside of me spoke: "Just go." So I did.

I emerged from a 21-hour plane ride and was catapulted into a new world full of lessons, patiently waiting for me there.

You Will Always Be Ok

It will feel like you won't and this feeling can linger for days and hours, maybe years. But when you least expect it, it will start to pass. And it will be more likely to happen when you finally learn to be ok during the times you doubt it ever will. Close your eyes and imagine the storm of all your suffering like the wind. Wind always, always moves. And this time in your life will pass too. When this moment arrives, be there, completely willing to let it go. It is getting you somewhere better than you'd ever imagine. You don't have to see it; you just have to believe it.

Changing Your Focus Will Change Your Life

Whatever we focus our energy towards will grow; whether it be the challenges in our lives or the successes. While at times it may be difficult to dig out of the trenches, we must find a way to focus on the light for that is the pull that will draw us nearer. It is often said that talking about our problems is our greatest addiction. Shifting your energy takes the practice of baby steps and the commitment to one day arrive at the place where it feels better to talk about our joys.

"I had to be forced away from the hyper-determination of eliminating my symptoms so I could see how life shifts as you shift your focus. Somewhere between the time I arrived in Delhi and the time I left, I went from an existence committed to "killing" disease to an existence committed to "healing" me. I had to acknowledge the parts of me that were saved when I stopped fueling "the war on Lyme"—for I was throwing the energy of a fight into my very own body."

You Have More Power Than You Think

You will realize that the only person victimizing you when you have the "victim mentality," is yourself. You will come to see that even though you might feel powerless, there is always something you can do to move yourself forward. You have to choose that something wisely though. It is not regurgitating your challenges to everyone who will listen and writing angry letters to all those who don't understand you that will move you forward. It won't be easy, but it is your job and until you are accountable for that job, you will always be waiting for someone else to fix you. As I learned, happiness never comes by focusing on all the wrongs in your life. It comes when you decide, despite all that has gone wrong, that you have the power to heal, grow, love and live.

It Is What It Is

There are two ways to look at the world: the way we think it should work, and the way it actually does. The struggle in life often comes when we fight the latter. Part of the secret of embracing the flow of life is the acceptance of the way things actually are.

Life will play out differently than you want it to and the more you expect that, the better off you will be. Being in control is an illusion that drains your energy, puts you on edge and makes you miss all the good stuff.

When we find a place of letting things and people be how they are, without the internal drive to change them, we come to a place of peace. Your family may not love you in the way you want them to, but it also may be the only way they know how. Your life may not transform at the pace you demand, but it might be for a reason you don't yet understand. In addition, some things in life just simply don't seem fair and that can be ok too. There is liberation in accepting the way things are, all while refusing to let it define how you feel. This is the elusive pot at the end of the rainbow: the gold of setting yourself free.

Suffering Has A Silver Lining

Suffering feels bad while it's happening. But, suffering also has a silver lining that never gets the credit it deserves. There are so many people, places and things that are found on our searches to 'get back to life' that we would never encounter otherwise. But most of all, crisis, as we often see suffering, is a way to purge that which no longer serves us

Suffering is almost always a stepping-stone to somewhere better. Failed relationships get us to the successful ones; illness helps us examine who we are and what matters; grief reminds us we are human and we can survive after inevitable loss; and the list goes on and on. You must acknowledge that suffering is often a catalyst for gigantic, beautiful change. And when you look at it that way, how can it be anything but perfect?

Letting Go Will Set You Free

You will have to let go in order to move forward. You will one day see that all that you tried to control, analyze and make sense of only tied up your energy. Feeling safe in the flow of life is essential to your health. It will probably be the hardest thing you do—surrendering to life instead of fighting against it. But when you succeed, you will find a new kind of safety that no changed plan or unexpected delay can shake.

One's path will unfold in its own time, revealing pieces of the puzzle only as they are ready. It will not always be in your time, but it will happen. The challenge is to show up, do the work, and peel away the layers. And in between, simply let go and trust.

You Already Know The Way

Perhaps the most important lesson of all is that you are the perfect compass for your own journey. After years of listening to the medical experts about my body, I finally did what I had not done so many times before: I began to listen to myself. I apologized to people in advance if

I didn't catch the negative being thrown at me. I respectfully reminded some that I did not ask for their vote. When I became grounded in my path, the spitfire around me just seemed to fade to the background.

I never came up with any "good" justification of why I should board a plane for a flight I wasn't guaranteed to survive to get an experimental treatment that might also kill me. But, I did it anyway. And, I did it anyway on the simple hunch that I knew it was what was best for me.

What I do know is that I've learned some essential lessons about intuition that I know will forever lead me to exactly where I need to be. I have discovered that sometimes the hunches that make the least sense are often the most important messages. I've found that ego and intuition do not pair well, so we have to release our fears of being wrong if we want that inner guidance to speak up with enough volume and confidence to grab our attention.

"I always thought I had flawed intuition, but I now realize I ignored it when it whispered to me. I was uncomfortable with making decisions based on anything, but justifiable data—a Virgo to the core. I soon learned though, intuition is far from logical. It calculates the answer and delivers it unapologetically, with no explanation."

As it turned out I would not only survive, but I would transform. The stem cells did in fact help heal my body, but what really saved my life were the lessons I learned along the way—lessons that catapulted my healing far beyond what any treatment ever could. And if ever you asked me then, if I thought I'd be where I am today—guiding others on this adventurous path of healing and spiritual growth—I'd laugh.

Really though, that is the glorious thing about life. It gets you right to where you need to be, even if it is a twisty, scary ride that sometimes seems to be going nowhere.

Bio

Amy B. Scher is the bestselling author of *This is How I Save My Life – A True Story of Embryonic Stem Cells, Indian Adventures, and Ultimate Self-Healing* (January 2013). With a history of chronic illness, Amy set out to discover the foundation of healing. She is an expert in mind-body-spirit healing. Amy uses energy therapy techniques to help those with chronic illness and those in need of emotional healing to identify, release and move on.

Amy is an Ordained Minister of Holistic Healing. She is a frequent contributor to national publications and healthcare blogs, and has presented to groups including the Department of Psychiatry and Behavioral Sciences at Stanford University. Most importantly, Amy lives by the self-created motto: "When life kicks your ass, kick back."

Visit Amy at www.amybscher.com

Chapter 4

20 Spiritual Insights From The Healing Matrix

by Jennifer Longmore

Lying in my crib as a baby, I can vividly remember orbs of light, seeing light beings, journeying into other dimensions and reflecting on why I had chosen to incarnate in this lifetime. As I developed language skills, I predicted events, communicated with 'imaginary friends' and delivered wisdom to the adults in my life.

My guides began visiting me more frequently and immersed me in their stories about such topics as parallel realities, cosmic dimensions, astral travel, the angelic realm, planetary shifts, and the language of light. These visits were a welcome and entertaining respite to the loneliness of being an only child.

By the age of three, my guides determined that I was ready to learn my soul purpose for this lifetime: to heal the masses as a direct channel for universal truth and to work with the most complex cases so that all could experience inner peace and thus create world peace.

I started receiving visions of my adult-self speaking to the masses about healing, equality, and world peace. Soon, I began to see my purpose play out in my own childhood reality. It seemed that everywhere I looked there was healing needed in the world: the starving children in Ethiopia, the foster children in my grandparents care, the stray animals on the street.....

I knew I needed to help but felt powerless in how to do that.

My only respite from this feeling of powerlessness was to do what I loved: play with my dolls and channel my inner need to nurture and teach them!

In hindsight, I wasn't playing with my dolls as much as I was role-playing my future. Each day, I would create a circle with my dolls and teach them about the 'meaning of life'. (So prophetic!)

I caught the eye of my kindergarten teacher who saw that I could already read and write. She asked me to read to the class (like a teacher) and invited school officials to the class to witness me 'performing' to my peers.

Having been raised in a spiritually open home, I didn't think of myself as "different" until that moment. It felt very uncomfortable, particularly because fitting in was so important to me!

From that moment, I spent the rest of my childhood and most of my adulthood dulling my light to avoid standing out and to avoid the commentary of what others thought of me.

I learned that in order to fit in, I needed to sensor my thoughts and abilities to make others feel more comfortable and become more accepting of me. Can you relate to this?

As the years went by, it became increasingly difficult to "know" things and pretend to others that I did not. "Knowing" things created a lot of internal conflict and I began to perceive myself as abnormal, and my intuitive abilities as a curse.

So I played it safe.

I chose a socially acceptable career path instead of following my heart and living fully on purpose (but I did make the most of it).

I went through university to become a social worker and began immersing myself in helping others in this conventional way.

I put myself through school by working as a counselor in developmental services and mental health, and as a trainer and advocate at a sexual harassment and anti-discrimination office.

This role seemed to serve my purpose, to a degree, but so often when not fully on purpose the Universe gives you a wake up call. So what did I get?

A car accident!

While I was busy with full time school and my various jobs, I manifested a doozy of a car accident. I had no choice but to slow down, to reflect and to HEAL!

Reiki was such a powerful healing tool in my recovery that I was compelled to learn how to use it to heal others. I needed to learn how to heal myself in order to help others to do the same! And that is exactly what I did!

So I got it, but I didn't quite GET it....

After I graduated from university, I began working as a forensic social worker, where I was assigned the most complex cases of child maltreatment, while also providing healing to services on the weekends. It is was an interesting juxtaposition to navigate such toxic situations during the week and channel such high vibrations on the weekend.

By age 25, given my exposure to spiritual dimensions, marginalized groups, and every form of child maltreatment possible, I had moved into a higher level of my healing awareness and abilities. There is little that you could tell me that would surprise me.

I know for certain that on my soul's journey, I needed to accumulate extensive knowledge in universal truth, child maltreatment, forensic pathology, trauma, inequality, dis-ease and healing so that I could empower others. Now I offer services that help others permanently heal their past, align people to their soul's purpose, illuminate their divine gifts and talents, and expand them into their divine essence so that they may be who they really are!

The decision to formally create a sacred space for this to occur via my healing business was a journey in and of itself. I needed to learn to get out of my own way so that I could confidently show up for others.

I had to overcome the fears of being seen doing 'new-age' work, letting people down, not being enough, and other such illusions so that I could really show up as a channel for divine love and light for the souls that were crossing my path.

I never expected that my business would be my greatest healer and that my clients would be my greatest teachers. After over 20,000 soul purpose sessions via the Akashic Records and 100's of classes on healing and ascension, I've created stronger boundaries, a healthier money story, and I've learned what it means to be a conscious co-creator and live in the question rather than the answer.

I've learned a lot about what healing is (and what it isn't), why some people heal and others don't, and it is still a lifelong learning journey. Here is what I've learned so far:

1. When you have a misidentified and misapplied sense of purpose, healing yourself becomes your purpose.

2. When you turn healing yourself into a full time job, it serves as an energy of distraction for living your life full out.

3. When you treat yourself as a project that needs to be fixed, this focus will always create more ailments to fix.

4. What you focus on expands. When you focus on what is wrong with you, you will continue to generate evidence to prove yourself right.

5. Focusing on what is 'right' with you frees an immense amount of energy to BE, to create, to move forward with joy and co-create an abundant, flowing, thriving life. Being your own best friend is the most precious gift you can give yourself.

6. There is always a spiritual root cause to any health concern. Connect with spirit for assistance with healing and witness an abundance of miracles.

7. A healer doesn't actually heal people - they create a sacred container for you to step into and create your desired shifts, if you so choose. You are your own healer. If someone claims to have all of the answers for you - run (fast)!

8. Healing is always a choice. You were gifted with free will, and in this space, there is no right or wrong, good or bad, it is all simply your choice.

9. Every healing opportunity has a silver lining. Cultivating deeper self-awareness allows you to identify what it is and be in gratitude (one of the highest healing frequencies).

10. We are all a work of art in progress - focus on the journey, rather than the destination.

11. The universe always has your back.

12. You are a manifestation of the creative life force energy (infinite, loving, and divinely perfect) and are created to allow it to freely move through you and touch everything and everyone that you encounter with that spark of light.

13. You already have everything you need.

14. You already are loved, accepted, and respected - abandonment, rejection and separation are all illusions. Oneness is all there is.

15. Illusion is the root of our pain and manifests as imbalance in our spiritual, mental, emotional and physical bodies. When you live in the reality of what is, you free yourself from the perceived 'pain' that holds you back from living in your fullest potential as an infinite being of light choosing an human experience.

16. Living in the question, rather than the answer, allows you to live in reality and create more expansion and possibility.

17. Time is an illusion and has no bearing on your growth - the present moment is your direct line to Source.

18. Striving for alignment to universal truth creates inner alignment. Universal truth is always evolving, just like you - enjoy the journey.

19. Your body has its own consciousness. Learn to listen to it and align with it so that you can stay in your body and be present to all of the opportunities and growth that can only occur through the spiritual vessel of your human body.

20. Be here now, fully grounded in your body, and make the most of your finite human experience. While it's fun to travel on your magic carpet, if you are leaving your body to avoid, create distraction, and go 'home' too early, you are missing the point. Your soul is infinite

and already knows all dimensions and beyond. There is plenty of time to play in the ethers and fly around at the speed of light. If you are meant to be there now you would already be there. There is a reason that your soul's wisdom chose a human experience and a human body to facilitate your soul's evolution, give yourself permission to enjoy staying in your body long enough to discover the magic of what that purpose is!

Bio

Jennifer Longmore, Forensic Investigator turned North America's Soul Purpose Expert, is the internationally acclaimed host of "Soul Purpose Central," 2-time best selling author, and creator of the popular Spiritual Leadership and Legacy Program and Highly Conscious Business Intensive.

For over 15 years she has been helping people remember who they really are through over 20,000 soul purpose sessions, including the who's-who of actors, professional athletes, CEO's of leading companies, and other influential luminaries. To learn more about how she can support you on your journey, visit www.souljourneys.ca

Chapter 5

A Spiritual Journey of Exquisite Self-Care

By Robin Hart

Life is a mystical journey at least this is what I have learned. Our perception colors the way we understand our life, as well as ourselves. Our journey is so much more than just the "survival boogie" or creating our goals. It's a journey of self-discovery and has the potential to be profound and fun!

We spend so much time missing out on being fully present. There are precious moments that we just take for granted. Have you ever been so wrapped up in something that you suddenly realized you have not even looked up at the beautiful sky? We have a tendency to go day after day without really looking around us. We put our focus on the past, and worry about the future. I have seen this not only in my personal life but also with my clients. I put myself in this category, because I have not mastered it yet myself. From my experience, living in the past or future is usually a painful state of mind. Either we are longing for the past, feeling guilty about what has already happened, or we are anxious and/or worrying about the future. These emotions affect the quality of our life and there is a physical price we pay as well.

As a society, we are now becoming more aware of the mind-body connection. I share this because everything is connected and we are not always conscious of the big picture. So you might be asking yourself; what does this have to do with life being a mystical journey? What I have discovered is that life is, whether we are conscious of it or not. What I mean is that we are always learning and growing; it is a natural part of our spiritual evolution. We are always expanding towards a greater understanding of ourselves. When we finally come to the place where we realize there is something bigger going on then we can go deeper into our soul's understanding. We must look within and realize that the only constant in our story is ourselves. This is where the spiritual learning comes in; we have a choice and can choose to step into the possibility of co-creating our life. We all have free will and no one can take that away from us unless we let them (and give our free will away).

I used to experience life as happening to me. I felt stressed and sorry for myself when things were difficult. I didn't take any responsibility for my feelings because I didn't know how. It felt like my life was out of my control and I felt powerless. We call this *victim consciousness*. I learned that this form of consciousness was the best I could do at the time, being who I was, with the level of understanding I had at that time. Once I realized that my thoughts and feelings affected my experience and how the world responded, my whole life changed. I realized that life was happening through me and my whole perspective changed as well. Something in me became very excited because I realized I had the power to change the way I perceived life and myself.

I began to experiment and play with my thoughts and feelings. I learned to look at the big picture. When we step back and can see the whole picture, that is when we get out of our own way for then we can see more clearly. This makes it possible to discover what our soul's learning is meant to be. Finding the deeper purpose in every situation is the key to personal growth and happiness. We have the opportunity to experience the Divine Play in our life. I believe everything happens for a reason and everything is in Divine Order. It may not feel like it at the time, but eventually it will be revealed. The key is TRUST; trust that something good is trying to happen and that there is a higher purpose in our life.

This is where we have the opportunity to tap into the mystical. When we look for the magic in life, from a simple rainbow to the deer in a roadside field, we have an opportunity to s-l-o-w down and remember the sacred in life. When we do this we tap into the feeling that there is something bigger to life than our daily to-do's. This helps us to step out of our selves so we can see the beauty all around us. This is how we connect to the magic of life.

We all have direct access to our higher power or God Source for guidance and clarity. We have been taught to look outside ourselves for the answers, but the TRUE answers reside WITHIN us. We have an innate ability to tune into our heart and bring our awareness inward. This is where we can access our TRUE guidance. I have experienced many chapters in my life, just as we all do, and I have discovered a lesson in each of them. I believe that we are spiritual beings having a human experience and if we choose to, we can experience this life as a spiritual journey of awakening.

My journey started as a young child when I was a natural counselor. I would bring home troubled children and try to help them. In my youth, the adults told me that I was an old soul. I remember this made me feel wise. I had a unique perspective as a child, which I believe has to do with the incredible childhood I had. My mother was an artist, musician and spiritual seeker. We had many wonderful adventures and I was exposed to an array of different types of people. I developed the ability to connect with people of all types. I discovered I was naturally empathic and I felt so much compassion for people.

As an adult, I chose the career of being a cosmetologist. It was a natural choice since I loved fashion and creativity. It was in my DNA; my grandmother had been in the business in the early 1930's. I've always enjoyed being creative and helping people feel good about themselves. Over the 26 years of being in this field, I did a lot of counseling with my clients as they sat in my cutting chair (they say hairdressers and bartenders are natural counselors). I found myself sharing and teaching my clients what I had learned.

On my journey of mastering the art of exquisite self-care, I studied self-growth and healing modalities. I had a wonderful spiritual mentor who worked with cognitive therapy as well as subconscious mind techniques. I learned a lot about myself and felt compelled to share it with my salon clients. Eventually, I participated in my mentor's 3-year ministerial program where I was able to go deep into my own spiritual practice. I also completed training as a Hypnotherapist and Rapid Eye Technician. I opened up a Spa and Wellness Center where I was able to offer services for the body, mind and spirit. I officially released the cosmetology aspect of my work to focus on helping people feel beautiful from the inside out. I became aware that helping people shift their pain into a bigger learning, fed my soul. I found that I enjoyed teaching the life principles that had changed my life even more than I enjoyed making people feel beautiful through cosmetology. I had found my calling and it truly fed my spirit!

Over the next several years, I created many programs, services and products to support and empower my clients. I was so passionate about making a difference in others lives that I would often become out of balance myself. My passion was so strong that I would push my body into exhaustion. I wanted to do it all; be a wife, a mother and a career woman. I would repeat this pattern many times. Sound familiar? Our society is so focused on "doing" that we have lost touch with *being* until I finally realized that I wasn't taking loving care of myself.

I began noticing this same pattern in my private practice (Anew Perspective Hypnosis & Coaching). My clients were pushing also and not taking loving care of themselves. So about five years ago, I began taking my women clients to the beach on nurturing retreats. These retreats have been so magical and rejuvenating and I have personally witnessed incredible transformations. I was incorporating all my personal learning as well as my professional training into these heavenly retreats; it is amazing how one thing leads to another on our life journey.

About three years ago, I began to feel an inner nudging to synthesize all that I learned over my lifetime and create the National Women's Holistic Lifestyle Institute. This experience of developing the Institute has taken my understanding of mastering the art of exquisite self care to a whole new level! What is truly amazing is that as I was developing this program, my own self-care was challenged. It is funny how it just sneaks up on you.

One of the most profound things that I've learned on this journey is that we are always evolving toward a greater understanding of our selves, and we are more powerful than we can imagine. There is so much love that resides within our heart and soul and we must learn to love and honor ourselves. I strive to be in the present each and every day, to practice what I teach, and to continue to learn and grow. I'm sure when I have learned all that I need to in this lifetime that this chapter will end and I will go on to the next adventure. In the meantime, I want to live in gratitude and take in all the blessings of life. My passion is to support and empower women & men in taking loving care of themselves as they discover the truth of who they really are.

Bio

Robin Hart is the founder and CEO of National Women's Holistic Lifestyle Institute and Anew Perspective Hypnosis & Coaching. She is a Minister, NLP Practitioner (Neuro-Linguistic Programming), Master Rapid Eye Technician, Spiritual Coach, Skills For Life Coach, Board-Certified Hypnotist, Flower Essence Technician, Reiki Master and Teacher. She is proud to be a member of the National Guild of Hypnotists – the largest and oldest hypnosis organization in the world as well as a member in good standing of the Rapid Eye Institute. She has a background in the cosmetology industry, where she contributed for over 26 years in helping women feel beautiful from the outside in.

Over the years, Robin continued her personal growth exploration and education in a variety of healing modalities. Eventually she opened *Anew Relaxation & Wellness Center* and later *Nirvana Spa & Wellness Center*. She currently works in private practice at Anew Perspective Hypnosis & Coaching as well as leading the National Women's Holistic Lifestyle Institute. She has had the honor of helping many women over the years to heal physically, mentally, emotionally and spiritually using healing modalities and products to support their body, mind & spirit, in order to live an exquisite life!

Chapter 6

The Journey of Awakening Happens in the Moment

By Angeline Johnson

Being spiritual is not a destination. It is a way of life. When you decide you want to do more, be more, command more, you will begin to awaken to your divine nature. It is a path of constantly learning about yourself and the world around you. It's a place where, moment-by-moment, you are faced with the decision to react or respond. You can choose an old pattern or possibly implement a new one. You can judge yourself and others or see their divine nature. You can choose to make decisions out of love or one's based in fear. Daily, these defining moments shape our lives, our bodies, and everyone else whom we meet. Let us now reclaim the power that is our divine birthright!

My Journey

We all have or will have a story of awakening. Once you have discovered your path, there is really no going back because your new awareness will only lead to more pain. My journey began in my mid 20's and like most, stemmed from pain. I had graduated college and moved to a new state where I did not know anyone and I was desperately searching to find my place in the world. Instead of landing a fabulous well-paying position as I thought I would, I wound up in a crummy job with crummy pay along with a crummy gambling addicted boyfriend and a crummy car that was constantly breaking down. Fortunately, I made friends quickly and did not have a shortage of people to go out for drinks with. This was all I had; an empty life with shallow party friends. I find it is only when we are in excruciating pain that we decide to make a life-altering decision or plead to a higher power to show us the way. The answer often shows up in a series of events we term synchronicities. People and events will show up in your life to offer you the opportunity to expand, heal, and get more in tune with your higher self. Sometimes what shows up does not seem positive at the time but down the line, you will have a clearer understanding of the part it played in your development.

My awakening began during this very difficult time where I would often lay awake all night calling different casinos searching for my boyfriend and showing up to work the next day exhausted. At the same time my grandmother, whom I was very close to, passed. I remember being at her funeral and someone brought a stuffed bear that was playing a melody. I had never heard this melody before but every time the bear played the melody I had this feeling as if my grandmother was trying to give me a message. Then, after returning from the funeral and going straight to work, a co-worker asked about the funeral. At that exact moment, the melody that the bear was playing came on the radio. I was completely in awe and knew instantly that it was somehow the doing of my grandmother.

Then, more amazing things began to happen. While I was lying in bed at night, I started feeling an overwhelming feeling of love like nothing I had ever experienced in my life. I would immediately begin crying but it was not tears of pain, it was tears of joy. Then, the top of my head would begin tingling with a sensation I had never felt before. Having nothing to relate this to I also thought that this must be my grandmother's doing. As the nights rolled on, the experiences became increasingly intense to the point that I no longer believed it to be my grandmother but thought it must have been a direct experience with God. Having no religious affiliation or spiritual upbringing I really had no basis from which to explain these experiences. At the time, I had no one in my life that I could possibly explain what was happening so what did I do? I "googled" it! I googled, "head-tingling" and a variety of other phrases trying to find others who have had similar experiences.

Finally, I came across, "Signs of a Spiritual Awakening". Immediately I though OMG that's it! I'm having a spiritual awakening! Now, what the hell is a spiritual awakening? Instead of being fearful, I was excited! It was a shout out to the universe and I was like, "Bring it on Baby"! And boy did they bring it all right. Within no time, I left the crummy job, the crummy relationship, sold my crummy car and up-leveled myself to a less crummy job, relationship, and vehicle. Because as I have found that is how it works... until you have learned the lesson you need to learn and change your patterning and vibration, you will keep attracting similar experiences.

Awareness of Purpose

Then, the turning point came. It was the one decision that I believed changed my course and put me onto what I believe to be my mission or higher calling. What I have found is that the higher call is so subtle that if you're not paying attention you may miss it. Mine started as a phone conversation with a friend on how I could locate a business-networking group. I visited the website and instead of finding a networking group, I found a meditation group. I saw the instructor's photo and in that instant, I knew I was supposed to go. I realized I had just experienced the higher call. And it was my intuition that was guiding me. I felt absolutely compelled to be there. I was so excited!

My boyfriend, coming from a very religious background, was immediately opposed to this idea and tried everything possible to convince me not to go. But my mind was made up and I was doing it. I attended the next meeting where I was introduced to meditation as well as the concept of energy healing. I had never heard of this before and I felt an immediate thirst for more knowledge and experience. I was also blessed to now have a mentor to help me navigate the process.

Within a few months I started having this overwhelming belief that I was supposed to be healing people. I didn't know what it was going to entail so for about six months I was frustrated knowing I was supposed to create something but I didn't have a clue what it was. Then, a few months later I got a call, which was another one of those subtle moments that shifted my course. A friend in meditation said that she had purchased us a booth at the Mind, Body, Spirit Expo and that she wanted to see me out there healing people. I remember thinking, OMG, this is a big deal! I can't get out there right now, I still have no clue what I'm supposed to do! I didn't know that this was exactly what I needed to trigger it all.

I got off work that evening went home and decided to do a meditation and see if I could get answers. I closed my eyes and not a moment later, I saw what I was supposed to be doing. I was shocked at how fast this had come to me. Then the next night, I decided to go into meditation to elaborate on what I had received. Once again, it immediately became clear. I received the basic process I would be doing and rather than over complicate it with too many thoughts, I decided to put it to work. I called my friend and asked her to meet me after work. The next day we met and were amazed and overjoyed as the process had a profound impact the very first time. I went to my mentor and showed her the process. She was also amazed by my sudden ability and we decided to offer it to the meditation group so we could analyze individual results. Since we usually had a small group, we decided that I would spend about 15 minutes with each person.

Delighted and surprised by the opportunity I found that the Universe wasn't done yet. Instead of a few people showing up there were about 40. Immediately, I knew that I was going to have to do a group clearing although the idea had not even occurred to me prior to this. So here we are just a few weeks after me creating this clearing process and I'm working with a group of 40 people. The catch was I didn't even know how to explain to the group what I was doing because I still didn't know what I was doing. All I knew was that I was absolutely certain that it would work. I was building the plane while I was flying it but I had never once experienced that amount of certainty about anything in my life. I had so much faith that it created a space for miracles to occur and they did. Committing to this path is what really kicked off the transformation process for me. I had decided that I was owning being a healer and that I would dedicate myself to assisting others in the process.

My Secrets to Rapid Transformation

This is the point that I would like to offer about what I have learned and what a few of the key distinctions have been for me so far. In doing this, my goal is to help guide you through what can be a scary, unusual, and life changing transformation period. Many people are just awakening and like I once did they have nothing and no one to talk to about their experiences. I know that by the fact that you are reading this that you have embarked on the journey of awakening. As I write this, it brings tears to my eyes and joy to my heart because I am so proud of you. You are the one who has had the courage to step up, stand out, and show up to define you in this world of infinite possibilities.

The first noticeable change I experienced when embarking on my path was ridicule from close friends and family. This step alone can be one of the most challenging to overcome because our friends and family are generally our support group. But this is to be expected because when you make a change other people feel threatened by it. They may not know why they feel threatened but at the bottom of it lays their unwillingness to change. Because you have changed, they are suddenly forced to look at you differently, relate to you differently, and ultimately as you own your power, treat you differently. With my family, I experienced resistance of all forms from ridicule to fear for my well-being. I made a choice not to let it affect my process, which resulted in my having to cut off communication from time to time because I refused to let negativity enter my space of enthusiasm and positivity. At the very same time I embarked on this path I also had a falling out with my two best friends that I introduced to one another and they decided to team up against me. Other close friends either tried debating me on my beliefs, talked behind my back saying I was doing the work of the devil and so on. For me the choice was simple but it wasn't easy. I decided that from that moment on I was going to have to start eliminating relationships from my life that were either toxic, unbalanced, or not in alignment with my higher self. It is often said that you are the sum of the five people closest to you. If you want to live a fulfilled life, you must surround yourselves with others that are going the same direction and have committed their lives to a path of personal growth. After leaving most of my social circle, I spent a considerable amount of time alone, working on myself. I had no one that I knew of directly that I was interested in keeping company with so I started listening to telecalls and going to classes with the types of people I would want to surround myself with. Then, after several years, I found a mastermind group that I connected with which really expanded my ability to learn and grow. I am happy to say that now I only have fulfilling, loving, aligned relationships with the people that are in my life and the new ones that enter.

Which brings me to my next point and the most crucial thing for you to understand and that is the concept of vibration. Everything is energy and every being vibrates at a certain frequency. Our thoughts, emotions, and beliefs make up the range that we typically vibrate in. Everything in the universe is attuned to a particular frequency. It can be best described like a radio station. If you are tuned to 95.5 and what you want is tuned to 107.5 it will not be possible for you to have it in your experience. This is how the law of attraction works. You must raise your vibration to the frequency range of that which you want in order to attract it. The fastest most effective way to do this is through energy clearing. Energy clearing is my area of expertise and therein lies the root of transmuting all negative emotions, limiting beliefs, and behavior patterns that cause us to offer up resistance to persons and situations in the world around us. Like Michelangelo said when creating David: David was always there underneath it all, he just chipped away what was not him.

Wisdom is not having all of the answers, but constantly searching for the truth.

Bio

Angeline Johnson is a cutting edge speaker, mentor, and healer incorporating advanced energy clearing techniques with real world application for men and women around the globe. She is the creator of the Violet Flame Clearing and Angeline "Angel with an Edge" energy infused products. To learn more about her custom offerings for groups and individuals email her at info@angelineboutique.com or visit www.angelineboutique.com.

Chapter 7

Autism: A Fast Track for Spiritual Development

By April Choulat Huggins

For as long as I can remember, I was always a sensitive person. I was excruciatingly shy, but combined with significant early childhood trauma, it was a recipe for high anxiety and selective mutism (psychiatric disorder in which a person who is normally capable of speech is unable to speak in given situations or to specific people). In my early years, I did not speak at all at school and took refuge in my art and in books. I did not know it at the time, but looking back I realize I could see the Truth by reading people's energy. So when adults in my life chronically lied to me or to themselves or had negative intentions despite an apparently positive outer façade, it was very confusing. I frequently saw one thing energetically, but was told and shown another thing physically. As a result I learned very early to doubt my own impressions despite the fact that most of the time my impressions were true and accurate. I always had a feeling that grown-ups didn't have a clue what they were doing. I felt old and wise and had a sense of just waiting until I was of age so I could be on my own and do what I was really here to do, without adults slowing me down. It feels a little strange to write that, but it is true.

When I was 19, I began working with children with autism, and that set me on my right path. I studied and mentored with some of the best innovative thinkers and clinicians in the field. I learned the conventional behavioral approaches, and when those weren't enough, I began exploring more innovative methods based on the latest research. I worked my whole professional life to gain a deeper understanding of the root causes of perplexing behaviors so that I might be more effective with the children I work with. In the beginning, I started from the outside by supporting the family system, and gradually moved more inward by looking at the function of the brain and nervous system. Never in my wildest imagination did I dream I would be shown the deepest origins of autism, which is occurring on the soul level.

While I have always been very sensitive to energy, I experienced an extraordinary spiritual awakening at the age of 29 when I lost my husband to suicide. It was through a series of events following the aftermath of his death that my senses heightened, I began to perceive waves of energy and experience spiritual healings with myself and others who crossed my path.

Shortly after his funeral, I began a training program to address sensory symptoms of autism. I participated in an internship and was expected to observe my trainer and take notes. During this time my nervous system became acutely sensitive to light, sounds, smells and touch. I started having problems with technology and my supervisor insisted I stay twenty feet away from her computer and electronics because they wouldn't work properly in my presence. I distinctly recall reaching for a light switch during this time and a blue arc of electricity extended from the wall to greet me.

I also began to experience vibrations in my hands and my energy centers throughout my body. I saw images of chakras and meridians and various other things I had no professional training in. As my training continued I would often, upon meeting a new colleague or student, feel my hands buzzing and like magnets, they would pull me towards another's energy field. Physical and emotional healings occurred. I spontaneously received spiritual information about children whom I had never met before and were not my clients.

I started to get information on a soul level regarding the origin of some of the children's challenges. As I received this information, I wanted to test it, to make sure it was not subconsciously created. I knew I wasn't imagining things for two reasons: other people were witnessing and experiencing it, and I began to receive data that I had never seen or heard of, or even know was possible. The rational side of me wanted to be as scientific as I could, to disprove information that was scary and which threatened my whole (rational) understanding of the nature of the Universe and my own existence. I began to draw diagrams and charts of information that was coming through me about an incoming client whom I had never met before. I did not read the client's chart until after I had completed writing down the information I received.

Information that came through regarding one child in particular showed a soul being shared by two bodies. (I didn't even know this was possible and had never heard of such a thing). I thought surely this must be a mistake. As I read the child's chart, I learned that he had been a *failure to thrive baby* and that he was a twin. This really got my attention – was it possible a child could fail to thrive because its body contained two souls? I theorized what could be happening here – is it possible the twin had received more Life Force than the Failure to Thrive baby?

I observed the client's session with my trainer as usual. This particular child was at the end of the program and would no longer require services. The parents were overjoyed at the progress he had made in such a short time. When they brought this boy in he was developmentally lagging and struggling; now he was in kindergarten and doing really well. Mom pulled out a photograph of the boy and his twin. When the boy saw the photo, he suddenly began to cry. I felt an enormous sadness in my heart and didn't know why. Then, the mother began to tell a story that no one in the room had heard. There had been a third baby. It had been a difficult decision and obviously was painful for the mother to tell the story. This baby had some birth defects and they had to terminate the pregnancy. Then, I suddenly knew – *that* was the baby that shared the same soul as the child before me. That was why this little child had been a Failure to Thrive baby. *Wait a minute, why am I being given this information? What am I supposed to do with this? I didn't sign up for this. I am here to learn how to enhance neurological functioning.*

"*But you did sign up for it?*" I heard a voice say.

I am a rational person. I while I am an intuitive, I also like science. I study neurology, psychology, nutrition, child development, and human behavior. I majored in Communication Sciences and Disorders and graduated with a 4.0 GPA. I see the big picture but I also tend to think linearly. For a long time I also fell into the trap of "Either/Or" thinking.

Either I'm scientific or I'm spiritual. (Which to meant, *Either I'm Normal and Sane or I'm Crazy.*)

Either I'm an Autism Specialist or I'm a Healer.

Either I work in modalities based purely on science or I'm "airy-fairy".

What a relief to finally realize there doesn't have to be an "either/or" way of looking at things. There is another way. It's "AND". I'm a healer AND an autism specialist. I am intuitive AND scientific. I am creative AND a brainiac. I can be a grounded critical thinker AND trust guidance from Spirit. I am a Wayfinder, as Martha Beck would say.

I struggled with this for a long time. I couldn't integrate my new identity that seemed to change overnight. I didn't know what to do with these gifts that had opened up in such an extraordinary way. My mind wanted to control it and figure out how to explain it. The fear to come out of the spiritual closet was immobilizing for me. Will it negatively impact my business if people really knew who I was? Will I outshine other people in my field that I respect and have learned a great deal from? Will people I love, who live in a state of fear of the unknown, shy away from me? Or worse, will they condemn me?

I sought spiritual teachers and energy healers and trained in different modalities. I learned practices that have helped me control my abilities so they do not overwhelm me with a cacophony of input. I have even more empathy for people with autism as I can relate to being on a different energetic wavelength, attempting to function in a plane of existence that sometimes feels too low of a vibration.

I used to have an overpowering fear of really being seen. It is not completely gone, but it is 90% gone. It has been a process for me to come to terms with the fact that I am a Healer, something that there is no place for in western civilization. Martha Beck describes this phenomenon well. She says that in Western society we separate the roles of mystic, doctor, storyteller, artist, therapist and herbalist into distinct professions. We don't have one word to categorize a person who is all of these things. In pre-modern cultures the elders would identify a child who demonstrates certain attributes and train him or her to be a shaman or medicine woman. If only I had been born into a culture that would have taken me in and shown me who I was at an early age, how my life would have been so much easier so much earlier!

All my life, I have felt very different and alone because of how I perceive energy and the supernatural side of life. I have come to realize there are many others experiencing the same thing. I discovered along the way that there are many professionals in the autism field who are using their intuitive and healing gifts. They are teachers, therapists, and doctors. They are in counseling professions and medical professions. They are the professionals who have waiting lists and who get the results no one else seems to get, those who seem to attract the most difficult cases.

No one wants to be the first to come out and say they have experienced miracles or that they regularly perceive angels and have an awareness of energy beyond the 'normal' spectrum. (Speaking of which, did you know some people with autism perceive the UV spectrum of light, like bees do?) It is easy to believe the child is the one who needs to be "fixed", "cured", "recovered" and therefore healed. What if autism is a fast track for spiritual development? What if we reframed the way we view such conditions? Are we helping ourselves by stumbling headlong into a tunnel of desperation in search of the cure without taking into account what the purpose is to all of it, what we value as meaningful in our world, and how we define quality of life?

For a long time I operated from a place of thinking somehow my human mind knew better than Spirit. In the beginning, I resisted my purpose and calling. The more I resisted, the more things went wrong and the sicker I got. Conversely, every time I've trusted Spirit and taken a step forward, things worked out exponentially better than when I attempted to control or wrestle an obstacle by myself. When I realized this, I decided to put all my faith in Spirit and to move forward on the path put before me, despite not knowing the end result. I have let go of attempting to control, and instead decided to step into Flow.

What a relief to know I don't have to have all the answers. I don't have to have it all figured out. All I need to know is my immediate next step and I will be supported, guided and taken care of. And so will you. What is your next step?

Bio

April Choulat Huggins, founder of Pathways Developmental Learning Center, integrates her spiritual gifts with her understanding of neuroscience to facilitate development of the maximum potential within each of her clients with autism spectrum disorders.

Her interests and professional activities have been diverse, ranging from travel and conscious living to neuroscience and spirituality. April works with families who have children with neurological challenges, as well as the professionals who support them. She has co-authored two book chapters in Dr. Steven Gutstein's "My Baby Can Dance" and travels internationally to share information regarding innovative autism therapies. You can reach her at april@pathwaysdlc.com.

Visit April on the web at www.pathwaysdlc.com and www.transcendautism.com

Chapter 8

Breathe Together in Harmony and Envision a New Future

By Sally Reed

My first experiences with New Age spiritual thinking began in Hawai'i. In the 1970's, my crazy wonderful aunt, began her awakening as she experienced a new consciousness that revealed the need for spiritual transformation. Turning 50, she gave up her middle class life, including her business and marriage and began studying Handwriting Analysis and the Spiritual Science of Letters and Numbers. Soon she started going by her new name of Hobrey H Z Brougher, based on the unique vibrational pattern that this combination of letters provided as a way to support the changes in her life.

The story goes that when Auntie Hobrey arrived on the Big Island of Hawai'I, she lived in an abandoned pineapple shack. She connected to one of the original New Age intentional spiritual communities and expanded her mind in every way, seeking clarity in this newfound space. I never indulged in the psychotropic drugs because that never resonated with me, but during my visits to this magical community, I embraced all the new insights that came from expanded consciousness.

As a sheltered daughter of the Midwest and a granddaughter of the Depression, I was totally blown away with sheer amazement at all this New Thought. This was not thinking outside the box; the box was nowhere to be found. I grabbed onto Auntie Hobrey's coattails, or should I say the hem of her muumuu, and began to ride the wave of unity consciousness. Each time I crossed the ocean and stepped into the magical world of Ahualoa, on the side of an active volcano, in the Rain Forest of the Big Island of Hawai'i, I began to awaken. I learned to live the question, what if I really could move ahead into a life of more love, joy and creativity, instead of allowing struggle, lack, and fear to be my teacher?

Auntie Hobrey had a mind like a laser beam, honing in on any judgments, misbeliefs, or unconscious behaviors. In the beginning, I was so stuck in the limited thinking that seemed to be the automatic default setting of my mind. I practiced returning to the present moment each time I would get distracted in order to release judgments and conditioning from my past. I learned to access higher levels of consciousness, the beginning of what we call ascension. I had plenty of experience with the unlimited; only it came in the forms of anger, fear, grief and lack. It just seemed so frustrating and was no fun at all when Auntie Hobrey would turn into a movie-like character that relentlessly pushed all of my buttons and brought up all my unresolved conflicts. She often pushed me to my limits and beyond. Upset and reset, she used to say. All the upset had me asking, where was all the peace and happiness and abundance?

She wouldn't stop until I got it. Got what? The ultimate challenge was to stop looking outside myself for validation, stop blaming any outside circumstances, and to look within. She drummed into me that everything was a gift from the Universe and happened for a reason, for my benefit. Look for the lesson and learn it once and for all. Stop judging yourself. Let go of self-disapproval. My task was to remember that I was an infinite Being of Light. I was learning to take full conscious responsibility for everything that was happening in my life and in my world. I became empowered to create my life consciously instead of unconsciously. I did not agree with all of her tactics, but I am eternally grateful for Auntie Hobrey's efforts to wake me up and engage me in a new way of being.

One of the original members of this Ahualoa community, my friend Joyce, tells me this first wave of "wayshowers" arrived in Hawai'i in the early 1970's from the world of academia. With clarity of purpose, their plan was to use their spiritual and anthropological knowledge to create an alternative inclusive community that recognized, valued and honored differences and to be of service to the world. They were known as the Fourth World Family. Joyce describes them as a group of loving, grateful beings doing planetary and cosmic work by opening and grounding higher vibrational energy and creating an affirmation that produced love, family, friendship, spiritual community, shared ventures and adventures.

Then there were the fascinating Forest People who lived up the road. My friend Connie has returned to the land that was purchased for their communal living experiment. Connie explains that they believed a radical departure was required for change to take place in the world, clearing the old to make way for the new. The Forest People were all about expanded ideas of sexuality and freedom and women's liberation from patriarchal dominance. They expanded their minds to include the radical idea that loving more than one person was natural and that jealousy could be transcended, by releasing judgment while respecting and listening to one another. Even though their lives evolved away from the experiment of living communally, being honest and open and clear is the work they continue to do for the planet.

One of my lasting memories is my second visit to Ahualoa. It was Easter and my 22nd birthday and once again, I was filled with grief. A triad of losses starting with the passing of my beloved mother to cancer, my best friend in a car accident and my father to a brain aneurism led me to escape to the healing environment of the islands.

With a sigh of relief, I returned to the grace of Aloha. Lifting my spirits, the smell of wild ginger wafted through the air as the Ahualoa community arrived at Auntie Hobrey's house to celebrate Easter. I can still vividly recall how they wrapped me in unconditional love, fed me organic fruits, vegetables, fresh eggs and my friend Theresa's famous and fabulous homemade whole wheat sour dough bread. For perhaps the first time in my life, I felt fully nourished and nurtured in mind, body and soul.

During that same visit, Theresa and the gracious Grethe introduced me to creating sacred space and the traditional structure of casting a circle, calling the directions, grounding to the crystalline energy of the Earth, connecting to the Nature Spirits and the Light from Source. Both women embodied the beautiful image of the Divine Goddess within, as they welcomed everyone with a song and a prayer. I breathed it all in.

Grethe also introduced me to Flower Essences, which are home-opathic remedies holding the individual flower's vibrational signature. Flower Essences are a living, energetic gift from Nature used as a remedy to heal negative emotions and promote higher frequencies. I begin to catch a glimpse of a new future filled with more possibilities than I could ever imagine.

It is time for all of us to prepare for our lives to change. The new future envisioned by the conscious Ahualoa community has arrived. Some may have been feeling a little lost as we leave the old way of doing things and move into the new multidimensional world that we is all around us. No matter where you are on your spiritual journey, you can continually align with love by clearing and releasing old wounds, old memories, thoughts, feelings, beliefs and behaviors that do not support you completely on your journey back to wholeness.

The ancient Hawai'ians had this all figured out from the beginning and encoded it in their language. Uncle Harry Uhane Jim says in *Wise Secrets of Aloha* that all life is a manifestation of divine energy and even the word Aloha means: "the breath of God in our presence". The five letters of the word Aloha reveal the Hawai'ian healing principles and call us to come forward and be in unity and harmony with our real selves and all life. A is for *ala*. *Ala* is watchful alertness and awareness. L is for *lokahi*. *Lokahi* is working in unity. O is *oia'i'o*. *Oia'i'o* is truth, honesty and authenticity. H is *ha'aha'a*. *Ha'aha'a* is humility. Ha means breath or Spirit. A is for *ahonui*. *Ahonui* is patience and perseverance. Now is our chance to breathe together in harmony.

The way to heal the past, reset those old dysfunctional default settings, and step into a new future, begins with the breath. New life always begins with that first breath of awareness. You might like to incorporate my 4Star breathing technique as a practical way to raise your frequency. Simply stop, bring your full awareness into the present moment and take a nice deep breath into your heart, into the center of yourself, your CoreStar. Breathe in all the love you need into every cell of your body. Then exhale as you open your mind, release your thoughts, and send your awareness down into the Earth, grounding into the crystalline energy grid of the EarthStar. Imagine that energy can enter through the bottom of your feet, filling you completely, feeling fully supported by the Earth below you. Next, send your awareness out the top of your head and connect with your SoulStar, your Divinity and your own soul frequency. Finally, let golden white crystalline light shower down from the AllStar, the Universal Source of Creation, filling you with love and life and light.

You no longer have to let the past define you. Let's all move forward and step into the light of new possibilities, breathing freely without expectation or judgment. We are all on the path of ascension now, creating a new world of community, harmony and equality that serves our highest good and the highest good of all.

Bio

As a Transformational Speaking Coach, Sally Holmes Reed helps authors, coaches, speakers, healers, trainers, experts and heart-centered entrepreneurs make a difference in the world while achieving personal and financial success. Sally uses her unique process called Inside Voice™ and her 4Star Breathing™ Technique to open up a whole new world as you learn how to access the creative part of yourself at the unconscious level. Clear any hidden conflicts that have been keeping you from getting more clients, making more money and creating the life you desire. Never again worry about freezing, fumbling or freaking out. Sally inspires you to speak from the heart and be authentic, be empowered, and be true to yourself.

Sally is an Author, BlogTalk Radio Host, Transformational Speaking Coach, Consulting Hypnotist, Certified Master NLP Hypnotherapist, Energy Healer, and a lover of Flower and Energy Essences. Since 2001, Sally has helped thousands of clients reach their goals through her private practice at Hypnosis Seattle and Akua Healing Arts. Now she is developing group programs and webinars to bring her work to the global community. Please connect with Sally at SallyHolmes-Reed@gmail.com. Sally also invites you to "LIKE" her on Facebook and get access to a free MP3 download of her 4Star Breathing™ Technique at https://www.facebook.com/SallyHolmesReedTransformationalSpeak-ingCoach

Chapter 9

Flow vs Force: How to Stop Overwhelm and Experience Effortless Success

By Melanie Benson Strick

As a little girl, my mom loved to tell me the story of when I was born. As the story goes Dr. Dagress delivered me out of the womb, turned to my mother and said, "You'll never have to worry about this one. She's determined to conquer the world. You could leave her in an alley and she'd figure out how to survive." I think my newborn mind must have seen that as a personal challenge. For the first 40 years of my life, I felt it was my obligation to figure out how to achieve the biggest dreams and outperform everyone I knew.

I turned to my greatest ally for this life challenge – my mind. I could count on my mind to solve any problem and help me strategize to achieve any goal. The only problem was I could not figure out how to turn my brain off. This super-tool of mine liked to solve problems at 4 am. During a massage, my mind would turn on and create super long checklists of things that needed to get done.

If I saw a friend or colleague leaping ahead in the game of money or success I would figure out what they were doing and try to replicate it. That little voice in my head would shout over and over again, "you're falling behind!' and I would kick into high gear to catch up. My internal processor had no "off" switch so any problem that came up I would think about a hundred different ways to make sure I left no solution stone unturned.

And it worked.

Mostly.

Until it didn't.

In my early thirties, I realized I was not a happy person. Being driven for more made me see how big of a gap I had between the life I wanted and the life I was currently experiencing. I tried so hard to make the gap go away. I set goals and did whatever I could to achieve those goals in record time. When I could not see how to achieve my goal in one direction, I would just find a way to remove the obstacle. I was like a bull in a china shop – if you got in my way, I would remove you. If I could not remove the problem then I would pull out all of the stops and work harder.

My strategy for success was to force, push or control my way to the outcome I desired. Unfortunately, the downside to force is exhaustion. I used up so much energy trying to manipulate, cajole and figure out how to get what I wanted that my body was constantly using up every ounce of power it had. Working seven days a week, ten to twenty hour days never seemed to be enough. My body made sure I knew that too... in my late thirties I developed adrenal failure and had to go on three-month disability.

My doctor, telling me that I was stressed out helped me see that my career was making me sick. My solution was to go out on my own so I could enjoy the freedom of self-employment. Little did I know that my force strategy would come with me and the cycle would begin again.

Two years into being my own boss, I realized I was still working 10 – 12 hour days, seven days a week. I had the pattern of being driven inside of me. If I wanted to feel better, I was going to have to get creative to heal my body.

I went to acupuncture and had needles stuck from my forehead to my toes. I tried re-birthing but the practitioner said I was a shallow breather. I spent thousands of dollars and weeks in therapy and personal development programs, talking about my problems (which didn't really seem to solve anything but at least I was aware). I attended spiritual mastery workshops and learned about my inner child. I had my eyes read and was told I was exhausted (which I knew.) After ten years, I had a library full of knowledge but still didn't have the answer I needed – how can I achieve more without being stressed out and exhausted?

Then my life turned upside down. My business crashed. The man I thought I was going to marry walked out the door. Most of my so-called friends disappeared and the million-dollar revenue stream I had become accustomed to dried up.

Almost overnight, my world became radically different. I pushed myself harder trying to come up with clever offers. I worked long hours trying to do more marketing. Nothing seemed to work. I felt paralyzed and stuck. The only thing left to do was surrender my force strategy in the hopes that a new paradigm would reveal itself to me.

That is when I discovered the key to real personal power: flow.

When you are in flow, life is easy and effortless. The best way to describe the flow state is to visualize what happens in a river. Water has the ability to flow around rocks (obstacles) while staying its course. Your flow state is much like you being like water, moving towards your ultimate outcome with a self-sustaining power to effortlessly move around obstacles. Like a magnet, when you are in flow, you easily attract into your life exactly what you need at the right time.

Achieving a state of flow is not something out there you have to learn. It is something that happens inside of you. It's a conscious paradigm shift that you must first see as possible then choose to activate in your life with these three steps:

Make The Decision

The first step in replacing force in your life is to decide is it the way you will live from this moment on. Perhaps your body has spoken and you feel exhausted. Perhaps you are looking for a new way to create success that doesn't result in feeling depleted anymore or you just want to thrive in your approach to achieving bigger goals. Either way, you must first decide that you desire to live a state of effortless flow in order to activate this more peaceful and sustainable approach.

When you decide that flow is the way you will live, you will be able to make better decisions and become aware of the places that you have unconsciously been using force to move through life. Awareness is essential to change your behaviors and create flow state.

Get Detached

A part of being in flow is learning to be detached. Being detached does not mean you don't set goals or have desires for new experiences. It means you recognize that your will doesn't always know what is best. Our ego mind is very strong and can often confuse material success with fulfillment. By practicing the art of detachment, you set goals but also know that you may end up somewhere else and that is okay.

This is where the mantra, "This or something better" has served me well. When you practice being detached the key is to get clear on the feeling state that your desired outcome would produce but let go of what it might look like in order to have it. For instance, in relationship, you might want to feel loved, adored and supported but you don't currently have that experience with your mate. Many people try to force that desired outcome from their current relationship.

However, someone in flow would let go of who it was that provided the feelings you desire. Instead, they know that by being committed to the energy of being loved, adored and supported it (those feelings) may show up in many ways such as through your clients, a child or even through a new mate. Letting go and becoming unattached does require diligence and can become a lifelong practice learning to recognize when to surrender.

Use Your Power Center

Your power center is located deep in your solar plexus. It is often referred to as your gut instinct or intuition. Often neglected our instincts are tuned to a different frequency than our minds. Our minds are usually caught up in how to get things done. When using your power center to make decisions you will learn to feel into your decisions instead of using your mind. Your mind can rationalize anything. Your power center will either feel expansive or contractive based on how well aligned an opportunity is with your flow state.

It is important to know what your flow state is in order to train yourself to use your power center. Many people are not taught to feel their feelings so they disconnect their mind from the rest of their body. Learning how to access your instincts may take some time. Your instincts also may require some fine-tuning. When I am working with clients the first step we always take is to re-establish what the rules for success are in their book. Once those rules are defined (I call them thrive factors) then the instincts can tune into the right flow of effort, resources and progress towards living the life you want.

Using your power center does require some new muscles. Often people, new to using this kind of evaluation, mistake contraction for a NO. Contraction simply means that the way you see this opportunity is currently in conflict with your flow state. That does not mean it's bad for you or the wrong direction. It means you need more information. When we are stretching and growing into new opportunities, it is easy to feel constricted. Do not stop evaluating until you explore why you are getting the constriction.

Recharge Yourself

Maintaining flow requires a constant recharging of your internal batteries, especially if you are a recovering "busy" addict. Many people have defined their success based on how much they can accomplish. Working long hours without a break not only will make you physically tired but you will also deplete your creativity. Creativity is the lifeblood of inspiration – without proper recharging it is difficult to continue to thrive and feel in creative flow. Burn out can cause us to make distorted decisions and lose sight of what's really important.

There are a lot of ways to recharge. Take a vacation. End your day at a reasonable time (and don't creep back to your computer late at night or sneak a glance at your smart phone.) Take weekends off. Set better boundaries. Eliminate toxic situations. Spend less time with people who drain you.

Choosing flow was the best decision I ever made. I'm happier, more peaceful and have found that by shifting out of my head and into my instincts, positioned me to recognize supportive resources I couldn't see when I was busy trying to get ahead. By choosing flow, I became more attractive and grounded. My boyfriend and I reconnected. We married on a beach in Fiji (more flow and a lot of surrendering created a dream come true.) I hope you will choose flow too.

Bio

Melanie Benson Strick, known as America's Leading Authority on Optimum Performance, has a gift for guiding fast-paced, overwhelmed, driven entrepreneurs to thrive in their small business. With over 11 years mentoring thought leaders and big thinking entrepreneurs, Melanie is liberator – uncovering costly breakdowns and de-railers while re-energizing profits– ultimately freeing the entrepreneur to do more of what they do best.

Melanie has shared stages across the globe with legends such as Jack Canfield, John Assaraf, Barbara DeAngeles and The Secret Millionaires James Malinchak. She is co-author of Entrepreneur.com's *Start Up Guide to Starting an Information Marketing Business* and *SMART Women Live Their Why*. Melanie's success tips are featured in magazines such as American Express OPEN Forum, Woman's Day, Parenting Magazine and the LA Times. Melanie is a proud lifestyle enthusiast and spends her free time in search of the best spas and beaches in the world.

Learn how to re-energize your business and get into flow with her free e-coaching series, 18 Tips to Re-energize Your Business in 7 Days or Less at www.successconnections.com/reenergize

Chapter 10

Awakening The Power Within; The Hidden Key to Achieving the Life of My Dreams

By Cindy Cohen

It was a warm and sunny day in Los Angeles, as I walked out of the grungy, depressing motel room. It may as well been dark and cloudy, for *me* anyway. I passed the reception desk, which was housed behind a wall of bullet-proof glass. As I approached my car, I glanced at the small group of homeless people who frequented the parking lot, each with all of their belongings piled high in shopping carts. They stared at me in confusion, as they always did. It was as if they were wondering, "what is *she* doing here?" Being tall and statuesque, I didn't quite blend in.

One last day with a place to sleep, I thought to myself. I could sleep in my car, but I had Derek to think about. Plus, everything we owned was packed into the back seat, so that wouldn't have worked anyway.

How did I get to this place? Why me? Is it just not meant to be? These questions had been haunting me for over a month now, ever since "escaping" that unhealthy relationship. There were never any answers though.

All of my dreams were down the drain. Maybe I should have just listened to what people back home had said—"you have a great job and a nice place to live; why can't you just be happy?" But I wasn't.

I had refused to settle for mediocrity. I had picked up two years earlier to move to the place I had always dreamed of living. I had other dreams as well. Dreams of writing a book, becoming a model, and one day helping women and young girls in some way. Helping women and girls, what *was* I thinking? It sounded so silly now, considering my circumstances.

I decided that on my last day in LA, I would need plenty of rest. After all, Derek and I had a long drive back to Ohio the next morning. I figured I could do it in two, maybe three days, tops.

I thought about how to break the news that we were leaving after picking Derek up from school. I had put it off until the very last minute, because deep down, I had hopes that something would "magically" happen to change things. Hopes that *somehow* we wouldn't be homeless and practically penniless. It broke my heart to have to go back, to show him defeat, but he deserved better than *this*.

"What will this do to him?" I wondered. Will this be a lesson for him to give up on his dreams? Will it scare him into never taking chances?

I walked into the bookstore and went straight to the fashion magazine section. It was a habit ever since I was 15, with dreams of becoming a model. Now, I was a little over double that age, and there I was, still with that dream. Still pouring over the pages of fashion magazines.

I passed by a table of various books and one caught my eye. Not sure why, but I was immediately drawn to it. I picked it up, headed to the back of the store and curled up in a chair. I glanced at the title, *Your Sacred Self.*

The first chapter talked about things like "Divine Energy" and "connecting to your Higher Self." This was all foreign to me.

I still had some time until I needed to pick up Derek, so I decided to read a little more. Then, there it was. The quote that forever changed my life;

"No matter how much I protest, I am totally responsible for everything that happens to me in my life."

As I read the sentence a few more times, I felt a strange, unexpected excitement. The answer to those questions that had been haunting me was right there.

I thought, "I am totally responsible for all of my struggles, unhealthy relationships, poverty, and now homelessness. Therefore, it wasn't my "fate" as I always believed. I *created* it. And if I can create all of those horrible unwanted circumstances, imagine all of the *wonderful* things I can create!"

Something changed instantaneously in that moment. The dark cloud that had been hovering over me seemed to vanish. It was a huge awakening. I went from being a "victim of my circumstances" to a feeling of empowerment. It's amazing how a shift in your mindset can dramatically change things.

I bought the book without hesitation, even though my funds were limited. I practically skipped to my car, filled with excitement, and having faith that everything was going to work out.

When I picked my twelve year-old up from school, I decided not to tell him about the plan to leave the next day. I had a strong knowing that it wasn't going to happen after all. I trusted that inner voice, my Higher Self—the one connected to Source or God, when having unwavering faith. I didn't realize that's what it was at the time. Being connected to Source wasn't even language I had heard before this book.

That inner voice was right. I got a call that very evening about a job and a place to stay.

Looking back, something "magical" did happen that day. I shifted my fearful, deprivation and hopelessness thoughts to recognize the divine connection that exists within me. I learned that while we all possess this divinity, it usually remains untapped primarily because of conditioning.

Life had now become an adventure, rather than the daunting struggle it always seemed to be in the past. My spiritual growth continued as I made every effort to stay consciously connected to my Higher Self, no matter the situation.

I discovered that the Higher Self is infinitely wise, and transcends the limited perception I had of myself. I recognize when I am in alignment, by paying attention to my thoughts and feelings, in any given moment or situation.

When I feel feelings such as love, acceptance, joy, harmony, happiness, peace, or faith, I know that I am living from my Higher Self. I have learned that when I am living from that place, anything is possible!

Miracles started to happen around me. People and resources started to show up right when I needed them. I got into the real estate business, and the first million-dollar sale practically "fell into my lap," within weeks of getting my license. Unexpected residual checks from acting gigs I worked a couple of years earlier started to show up. Life seemed to flow with ease.

Also living from that place of "believing anything is possible," I immediately reclaimed my dreams—dreams of becoming a published author, professional model, and even the dream of one day helping women and young girls.

When I was 15, I would picture myself walking down a runway in front of hundreds of people. I began to revisit that picture. It was just as crystal clear and I felt just as much excitement as I did back when I was a teenager. It was so real in my mind's eye—I had no doubt that the picture I saw would become a reality.

I thought about Derek, and knew that having a modeling career could possibly take too much time away from him, so I decided to wait until he left for college. I did not let the thought of my age deter me. I would be 39, which most would think laughable, as anything over 25 is considered ancient in the modeling world. I refrained from sharing my dream with anyone, as many did not believe in my new mantra, "anything is possible."

I did not know the *how*, only that I envisioned myself signing with a top-modeling agency. I knew that the one or two ideas I could come up with were no match for the Universe and its *infinite* ways of making things happen. I had faith that the path would be revealed when the time came—the right person or opportunity would show up that would lead me closer to realizing my dream. I just had to be ready, recognize the opportunity when it presented itself and take action. I would definitely be ready, as I had prepared for this dream since I was 15. I lived it breathed it, and studied everything about it.

A few years went by and I met and married my wonderful husband, Simon. On one of our early dates I went to his home for dinner. When I spotted *Your Sacred Self* on his bookshelf, I knew he was someone I could share my dreams with, and I did. Shortly after, I wrote and published my first book, *The Life of Your Dreams*. It quickly became one of Amazon's Top 50 Books on happiness.

Before I knew it, Derek had graduated from High School. We planned a cross-country trip that would end with us dropping him off at college.

Then it happened.

I was surfing through the TV channels when I saw a commercial that changed everything. It was announcing upcoming auditions for a TV show, casting women over 35, who had unfulfilled dreams of becoming a model. I had goose bumps.

I knew this was *it*! This was *the opportunity* that would lead me closer to my dream.

After leaving Derek at college, I took action. At the age of 39, I found myself auditioning for the Reality TV modeling competition, She's Got the Look. Out of thousands of women who auditioned, I was one of the 20 chosen to compete in New York City.

After 5 weeks of filming, while competing in various challenges, I was the last one standing, and was crowned the winner of the show. One of the prizes included a contract with one of the top modeling agencies in the world.

Appearing on the show led to worldwide exposure, which resulted in many women seeking me out, wanting help changing their lives and achieving their dreams. I recognized that it was yet another opportunity presenting itself, so I began working with many of the women who contacted me.

This was the start of my coaching business, dedicated to helping women and young girls achieve their dreams.

The world is full of people who believed in their dreams enough to take action, prove the naysayers wrong, and persevere, no matter what obstacles got in the way.

They knew the first step was to make the decision. This is frequently the step that many people have trouble with. They don't make the decision about what they want because they get caught up in the "how." Being unable to see the possibilities in making it happen, they give up on their dreams. It's not important at this moment *how* you're going to get there. The first step is deciding what you want with as much clarity as possible. Can you picture it clearly in your mind?

They did the work required. Take small steps toward your dream every day. Get the skills necessary, do extensive research, learn everything you can, so that when an opportunity shows up, you are ready to take action.

They believed in themselves. You must have unwavering faith and adopt the mindset, "I intend to create this and I know it will work out." If you lack the confidence, go to seminars, seek out a mentor, or hire a coach.

They persevered. You never know when your opportunity will come—it could be tomorrow, or in 20 years. The more passion you have for your dream as well as knowing *why* you want to achieve it, will motivate you to keep moving toward it. Write down the many ways achieving your dream would change your life, as well as the lives of others. Your "why" should be so strong, that you won't give up, no matter what.

Bio

Cindy Cohen is a model, author, speaker and transformational coach. She worked in the field of research and development for eight years before giving it up to pursue her dreams. At the age of thirty-nine, she inspired thousands with her story on the TV show She's Got the Look, before snagging the grand prize of $100,000, a modeling contract and a spread in SELF Magazine.

Now running a successful coaching business dedicated to helping women and young girls achieve their dreams, she has spoken to and inspired groups of thousands. In 2011, she was personally hand-picked by Jack Canfield, America's #1 Success Coach, Creator of the Chicken Soup for the Soul series, and featured teacher in The Secret, to bring Transformational Training and Coaching to audiences worldwide. She is also a Certified NLP Coach, helping to identify and remove blocks that keep people from living their highest life.

Cindy's biggest inspiration is her amazing son, Derek, who will soon be pursuing his Master's Degree in International Studies. She lives in sunny Southern California with her husband Simon, and is an avid traveler. You can find her at; www.CindyCohen.com, or www.facebook.com/cindycohen

Chapter 11

Discovering A Doorway To Awakening

By Sharon Boon

I was sitting in the dining room of a woman's house that I had just met an hour earlier. I was sitting in a meditative position, waiting for my turn to receive my first Reiki attunement. I was nervous. I really didn't know what to expect. I looked around at the other people in the class; they were meditating while waiting for their turn as well. I went into a breathing exercise that I knew and cleared my head. At that moment, I heard a male voice say, "welcome home." I immediately opened my eyes. I didn't see anyone there who could have said that since everyone was female. The others in the class were still in their positions undisturbed and I knew, even though the voice was loud, it came from somewhere within me. Something dormant was awakening inside of me.

When it was my turn for my attunement into this Japanese healing technique, I told my teacher about what had just happened even though I risked her thinking I was crazy. She just nodded her head and said, "How wonderful." I received my attunement and finished the course.

Over the course of the following year, my intuition began to develop and for the first time in my life, I felt safe to acknowledge a hidden side of myself. In 2003, about a year after I took my first Reiki class, I threw myself into the study of self-development. For the first time, I felt I was on the right path. As I developed, so did my abilities. I began to use my intuition to help me in everyday life. I felt a connection to something far greater than me and with it, came the responsibility to use it wisely. I used it to help me make the right decisions even though I might want something else. In turn, I feel more connected, alive and at peace then I ever did before.

I had always used my intuition to help me with things in the past, but now I use it to help co-create my life. It has helped me overcome many fears and worries. I now know when I follow what my gut is telling me then things will be okay, that I am not alone and I can achieve what I want.

Years ago, I had been written off by the school system telling me that I would never amount to anything but now I knew I could do anything I set my mind too. This was all new to me and it was up to me to decide what I wanted.

All of these experiences I was having helped me learn a lot of life lessons over the course of several years, but the thing I learned that helped me develop my intuition the most was meditation; specifically, I learned how to keep my energy grounded and centered. This allowed me to keep my focus and be in the here and now (also called "being present"). This is so important because when you are constantly thinking or living in the past or possible future, you miss what is happening now. This is a sure way to lose your ability to listen to your intuition. Intuition can be very strong or very subtle so being present helps you notice when your intuition is trying to tell you something.

Also, as time went on, I came to understand the Law of Attraction. It became a focal point for me and helped me direct my attention to what I really wanted in life instead of what I didn't want. It helped me because it introduced me to synchronicities it has with intuition. This understanding of using our intention to have a say in the creation of our lives, brought me to a whole new level. I came to understand that practicing the Law of Attraction was not just a technique but also a way of living.

To give you an example of how this all works, I was telling a friend of mine about a book I had just purchased and during our conversation, I had the impression that he needed to read it too. Although he said he would look into it, Source (God, Divinity) had other ideas. As I was having my lunch, I had a feeling I should go out and get some ice cream. Ice cream in hand, I decided to visit our local thrift store. Walking through the book section, I found the exact same book staring me in the face. I purchased it and gave it to him that day. He was blown away and it just proved to me that following your intuition leads to synchronicities that can have a real impact, not just on your life but others as well. This was not the first time a situation like this has happened to me. It taught me to follow my instincts and understand that there is a higher power helping us and guiding us. By relying on it, I develop my intuition even more.

As my intuition grew, so did my understanding of how to create the life I wanted. This awareness changed how I interact with the world. Because my life had changed, there was no going back to where I was before. I developed a daily practice of gratitude that shifts my energy from negative to positive in mere seconds. Gratitude is a life changer. You cannot be mad and grateful at the same time. I knew if I wanted my life to change then I needed to be in a state of gratitude.

I begin each day by listing all the things I am grateful for. When I travel, I do the same and before I fall asleep. Gratitude keeps me in a positive mindset and helps me attract what I want in life. No longer do I attract what I don't want. This is one of the keys of the Law of Attraction.

Several things you can do to help you get more in tuned with your intuition is to stop and do a "check-in" process... clear your head and ask yourself, "How am I feeling at this moment?" Then ask, "How is my body feeling at this moment? Is there anything I need to know?" This should only take a couple of minutes to do. Over time you will start to get more in tune with your body and ultimately your intuition. Your body is like a receiver and it knows what is going on and what you need. The more in tune you become with it the better connected you will be with your intuition.

The next thing is ask for guidance from Source (God, Angels, Guides, the Universe, Divinity). Ask them for help to interpret what you are receiving from your intuition. I always ask, "Please intervene on my behalf and help me with _____." This has helped me build a stronger connection and helps me feel and know that I am safe and cared for outside of my human family.

Also if you don't trust your instincts, or dismiss it and find out later that you should have followed it, don't beat yourself up over it. Instead, learn from it and move on. I have dismissed things in the past and seen what I would have avoided if I had followed them. This is a live-and-learn process, and it can take time to understand how to listen to your intuition.

By following my intuition and practicing the Law of Attraction I've awakened to a whole new understanding. Since my first Reiki class in 2002, I've been exposed to a whole new way of living that I didn't know existed. I've taken more Reiki classes and received my Reiki teaching certificate. In 2010, I started a company to help others awaken as well. I now teach meditation and the Law of Attraction as a speaker, writer and life coach.

This was not how I thought my life would be. When I was told by the school system that I wouldn't amount to anything, that it was best if I learned a trade to find some way to support myself, it destroyed my ability to believe in what I could do. Reiki helped me awaken, to see my potential, and has helped me turn my life around. When they said I wouldn't go to college, I did. I have been able to achieve a lot more than I thought I could and I have done all of this by following my instincts and using the tools I learned to achieve what I want in life.

I am very grateful to the Divine, Reiki, that voice, the Law of Attraction and most of all, to my intuition who lead me to where I am today. When I heard that voice over a decade ago, I never knew that the journey would lead me to a happier, more fulfilling and prosperous life then I thought or was told I would have. With it came peace and knowing that I am loved and taken care of – I just needed to be open to receiving it. Reiki was the doorway that helped me awaken to my intuition and to a new state of being.

Bio

Sharon Lorraine Boon is a Certified Life Coach and alternative health practitioner. She is a writer and motivational speaker. She teaches Law of Attraction, Meditation and Reiki. Sharon is the founder and creator of Passage To Yourself, a company which specializes in helping people find and achieve their dreams and goals by removing conscious and subconscious blocks that stop them from creating the life they want. To learn more about Sharon you can do so at: www.passagetoyourself.com.

Chapter 12

Please Help Me To Be More Godlike

By Nancy Kaye

One evening after work, I prepared my specialty dish of linguini and clam sauce along with a delicious organic green salad fresh from my garden for my young girls. The three of us had a delightful evening, filled with the mundane routine of dinner, homework, baths and a bedtime story. After my children went to bed, I prepared for my nightly ritual. I worked in the field of fashion, as was the style of the '60's we all had BIG hair. I had to carefully roll the large, pink, hard-plastic rollers in my hair and attach each roller with long silver clips. As, I snuggled into bed carefully arranging my head full of curlers and started to drift off to sleep, I spontaneously said, "Please help me to be more Godlike."

I awakened at some point in the dark night by the most brilliant light I have even seen. I saw a beautiful radiant magnificent Angel looking down, beaming tender love directly into me. I was overwhelmed with amazement! Then I remembered my hair curlers, I had not expected company or a guest in the middle of the night. This is NOT how I greet guests. As that thought formed in my mind, I received the idea or message from the angel that she was not concerned with my hair rollers. She continued to look at me with unconditional love until her light shined so brightly I had to close my eyes. Soon after, I fell back to sleep.

My Angel's visitation haunted me... why did she visit me? I thought about this off and on throughout the day. I did know her visit was a direct response to my asking to be more Godlike. She was the answer. She was there, in all of her loving brilliance for me to see and know that she is real. I now knew that my request had been received and that she is there for me.

Puzzled for more information and answers, I sought out a psychic that a colleague had recommended. When I went to her house, she immediately took me to her backyard. An old tree had been struck by lightening. She told me she had prayed over the tree many times and proudly showed me the results of new green life and limbs growing out of the ash cavern and flourishing from the stump. I had never been to a psychic before and this story helped me to trust her.

We went into her living room and she allowed me to tape record her psychic reading of me. As I unfolded my angel visitation experience, she looked squarely at me and without hesitation told me directly that this vision was a part of me and that the Angel was me!

I was sure at the time that the Angel was a separate entity. I spoke again, arguing, how magnificent this being was, not to mention the love and beauty that emanated from her. I protested that she was about seven feet tall to my five foot two stature. I shared that she also and had inde-scribable otherworldly luminous beauty. My psychic replied that my request to become more Godlike was met by a living angel inside of me being projected outward for me to recognize her validity. She was an answer to my plea and was there to guide me in my Godlike quest. I patiently listened to her and on some level, started to believe; however, another part of me still had difficulty understanding that this Angel was really an aspect of me. My psychic also told me of many other amazing events to come into my life that I could not believe or even understand at the time; however, they all eventually happened, just as she told me they would.

She told me I would meet and be very close to a tall Indian man. Since I was single at the time, I could not understand being close other than dating or having a relationship such as being married. In right timing as only serendipity provides, I was at a huge New Age event and it turned out a tall Indian Man was the keynote speaker. I immediately recognized him as I had interviewed him for Chicago's Elite magazine when I was their lead writer. Swami Satchidananda became my Guru. He taught me about meditation and provided me a deeper under-standing of spirituality. He taught that truth is one and paths are many.

He would tell us, "Cosmic vibrations are there, but you have to have to tune in to the right station to receive them." The initiation, closeness and deeper understanding led me to become closer to God.

As I continued my spiritual journey, I began to understand that taking one step leads to another. Being receptive to and receiving our spiritual gifts moves us forward, deepens our understanding and uncovers more of who we are and who we are meant to be.

As I continue the process of increasing my attunement with and connection to our creator, I am better equipped to create and shape my own destiny. When I become receptive to my blessings, I continue to grow spiritually. Because of my spiritual experiences unfolding within me, I gain understanding and move closer to my highest self. With seven simple words, "Please help me to be more Godlike," posed as a request, I experienced a life-changing event.

This amazing experience propelled me to understand that my life mission is to be of service to help others unleash their highest individual spiritual life potential plan.

By sharing my personal life story and holding my client's hand with guidance all of the way, I can help them to find their new deeper life journey. I teach my clients to open up and ask, "ask and ye shall receive," as Jesus Christ taught. This is acknowledging that spirit is there in you and in all of us. This action step paves the way through uncharted territory for deeper life meaning. Omnipresent benevolent love from our creator is always to be found when we learn to tune into it. When this understanding sets in, it is very reassuring on life's bumpy road. When we actually experience Divine Grace, we are truly blessed.

The vision and space that I hold for my clients taking their quantum leaps, is similar to the caterpillar turning into a butterfly while sequestered in their cocoon. In the quiet, the caterpillar takes on a new form. The rebirth process moves them from gestation - releasing old forms and ideas - to the full-on transformation to create beautiful wings that carry them to places beyond their imagination to freedom. The art of listening for guidance and taking action in that direction will indicate the next step and help you adopt the flow of your blessings. When we practice gratitude, it magnifies our ability to receive our blessings.

This is truly a life changing experience.

All of my life I had searched for understanding of the higher realms of our creator. As single mom with two small children, I enjoyed a wonderful and lucrative job as a National Sales Manager in the fashion world and life was good.

Still, I found myself restless in search of something. I had all the material possessions, a lovely large home with a view, a new car, a successful career and happy healthy children. What more could I want? I could not ignore that I still felt the need the need to go deeper, find and connect with something beyond myself.

I needed to search within myself to find my deeper meaning. I needed to delve into my deeper spirituality and find more understanding of life.

In my quest for higher understanding, I had been a student of Yoga for several years and was interested in all of the world's major religions since early childhood. In elementary school, I would ask to go along with classmates and their families to experience their form of worship.

I carefully studied my friend's motions and copied their prompts to tell me when to kneel, pray, listen to the sermon or sing along from the hymnal when I was invited to their house of worship. It was not as if my family was un-spiritual. As a small child, in the family evening gatherings, there were lessons about God that my dad would read. Sometimes he would play the violin. The favorite family story was when I would say, "what will it be tonight God or the violin?" My father knew about many areas of Spirit. He knew of a higher power and had a deep personal spiritual understanding. He was a doctor and patients would report that he had visited them with healing in the night during their most hopeless times. Universal in his spirituality, he was happy to talk about and teach me all aspects of various religions and spiritual matters. My mother and he had the same deep spiritual understanding.

So, I was raised to be open to many spiritual ideas. However, I always wondered... holy books like the Bible (Old and New Testament), the Torah, the Qur'an and the Tipitaka all have references to Angels. The Bible beautifully depicted Angels with their lovely image of immaculate gossamer flowing gowns. They were always there to help humans in need, whether it was to guide, instruct or save them from harm.

All of the stories depict Angels as kind-looking with smiles and virtuous with their actions concerning human beings. Even as a young child, I wondered if Angels were real or if they only existed back in time when those holy books were written. I surmised, in my child's mind, that biblical times were so long ago that Angels might not exist in the modern world. My answer and the truth would come in person later in my life. How do we find fulfillment and thrive in the Spiritual Age? By going deeper into our soul and knowing the truth and remembering that our source and creator is pure love. We are never really alone. Trust and just ask for help.

Bio

Nancy's background includes hosting her own TV and radio shows in Chicago, New York and California. She is an internationally published writer (122 countries), having interviewed many famous people, including H. H. the Dalai Lama, Dr. Deepak Chopra, Dr. Wayne Dyer and many more. She is an engaging and inspiring keynote speaker.

Founder of The Confident Communicator™ Workshops, she instructs one-to-one personalized and group training re-programming sessions globally in all areas of communication. The intensive curriculum is tailored to the needs of each client. She diagnoses, evaluates, and teaches clients on a needs basis, and fine tunes them offering coaching, on-call client support, and empowerment.

Nancy is the founder of Define Your Destiny™ Intensives. She unveils the secrets to creating permanent change in your personal, professional and spiritual path. This unique self-development immersion Course with mentoring follow-up gives you the powerful tools you can use and build on throughout your entire life. Finding deep solutions to following your destiny to discover and live your perfect life plan.

Nancy is a Contributing Editor for the international Integral Yoga Magazine and heads the West Coast Bureau office.

She is the founder of Quantum Leaps Mastermind Group.

Chapter 13

The Ripple Effect of a Mother's Legacy

By Tina M. Games

One of my biggest spiritual teachers was my mother. The unfortunate thing is – she never knew it. And truthfully, neither did I – until she transitioned from the human realm to the spiritual realm.

It was this transition that magnified the power of my own understanding about **life purpose legacy** (everything happens for a reason). As her daughter, I was able to see how her life story affected my own.

As a *Life Purpose Intuitive*, I'm a lover of story. I love hearing people tell their life stories. Through their words, through their laughter, through their tears, I hear threads of meaning and of purpose. I have a divine gift for weaving these threads together in a way that unveils deeper meaning.

It's this meaning that brings the "aha" moments - the deep understanding combined with desired clarity that leads to divinely-inspired actions. It's this meaning that paves the way to choosing an authentic path of work. It's this meaning that helps us make sense of the relationships in our lives. It's this meaning that sparks the richness of living a life on purpose.

Even in the most difficult of times, there is light - and a deeper meaning, if we're open to receiving it. Every part, every experience, every lesson of our life story carries significance and paves the way toward fulfillment of our life purpose.

My understanding of life purpose deepened when I received an unexpected phone call in early February 2012 with the news that my Mom had passed away in the wee hours of the morning. I remember sitting there stunned, not fully aware of whether or not I was dreaming.

It was hard to imagine that a woman who had played such a big part in my life was suddenly gone.

My mother's passing opened my eyes to the reality that life could end at any moment for any of us – and when that time arrived, can we honestly say that we've given life everything we have?

Have we become all that we know we can be?

Imagine for a moment a pebble thrown into a pond. It creates ripples that go on forever. I believe that mothers are a significant part of the *ripple effect* of humanity – that will transform the world into a more loving, more nurturing place.

When a mother is living life with complete authenticity, she's subconsciously giving permission for her kids to do the same. She is truly at her best – creating powerful change for herself, her family, her community and for the world at large. It's all part of her *ripple*.

But what if something goes awry and her ripple stems from a place of frustration, confusion, disconnect or unhappiness?

My transformational work with mothers came out of my own experience of connecting with the moon during a really dark period in my life. Shortly after the birth of my first child, and after making some fairly significant life changes at the same time, I fell into depression – a place that felt so foreign to me, a place where I felt like I had fallen into a black hole with no way out.

It was during this time, a period that spanned over two years that I had disconnected from everything that made me happy. Because my son suffered from chronic illnesses related to serious colds and severe ear infections, I made a very difficult choice to give up a successful career in order to care for my son full-time. I hadn't realized until this experience how much of my identity was tied into my career. Without it, I felt lost and very unhappy.

No one understood the pain I felt – except my mother. She was the one person I could speak to without censoring myself and she became my confidante from that point on.

I also found myself falling back on a great passion of mine, journal writing. And as a mom of a baby who did not have a normal sleep schedule, I found myself exhausted and emotional much of the time. So night after night, after I'd get my son settled and after my husband went to bed, I'd grab my journal and retreat to my favorite chair… besides a big bay window where I caught a glimpse of the moon. It was the moon that taught me the meaning of transition. I'd watch this beautiful lunar goddess, night after night, move in and out of her various phases. And before long, I began to connect her phases with my own emotional tides.

I noticed that the moon always began in darkness and gradually, she'd move into full light – and cycle back around again. And I noticed the contrast between dark and light, the darkness of the night sky against the beautiful full moon light. I started connecting to this as if I was being divinely guided through my own transitions of dark and light. I began to notice the ebbs and flows of my emotions. There were good days and bad days.

So when I came to the point of writing my book, *Journaling by the Moonlight: A Mother's Path to Self-Discovery*, I wanted mothers to realize that every human transition begins in darkness and gradually moves into light, where we get a glimpse of what is possible. And then we retreat, to ponder the many ways we can manifest these possibilities into reality. This requires deep work, where we step into our own truth and into our own power and where we can emerge in the most authentic way possible.

This is what I call the Blue Moon phase – when we finally realize that we are here on this planet to be who we are; to put our personal thumbprint on the world in the most truthful, most authentic, most unique way possible. Each one of us is an individual, being divinely guided on our own purposeful path.

Because moms are natural role models, our kids are observing us all the time. There's a lot of truth in the saying, "Monkey see, monkey do." In other words, when a mom is modeling the value of following her heart, her kids get it – much more than they would if she was just saying it. Kids feel energy. They know when a person is happy and when they're not. So why not be happy and let the ripple flow?

Wouldn't the world be a much better place if we were all following our hearts? If we could truly live life with passion and purpose, everything would have a richer and deeper meaning. It would create a ripple of positive and loving energy that could literally heal the world.

Each and every one of us has the power to create great change in the world. This change has the most impact when we begin with ourselves. When we look in the mirror and honor the person who is staring back.

• Who is this person? Do you really know her at her core? If you were to remove every label that she wears – mother, wife, partner, community leader, business owner, loyal friend, etc. – who is she?

• Pretend for a moment that each of these labels are a blanket. Slowly remove each blanket, acknowledging the label it represents, and set it aside. Continue doing this until you have no more labels except SELF.

• Who is SELF? Take a moment to describe SELF from the inside out. How do you feel when you're not bombarded by what the world thinks you should be? What are your passions? What are your dreams? What makes you come alive? How does this person – from the inside out want to show up in the world?

These are great questions to ponder in your journal, allowing yourself to answer them truthfully and completely.

When we start chipping away at the exterior labels, what do we look like on the inside? What is our "diamond in the rough?"

Once we discover this, we've connected with our authentic self. And it's from this place where purposeful, powerful and magical ripples are created.

What kind of ripple are you sending out? Are you noticing the flow of your own energy and the impact of your emotional tides?

When we take a close look at our own life patterns and the many lives we touch within our own ripple it's a real eye-opener!

I saw my mother's ripple quite vividly at her memorial service. As I stood there in conversation with the many people who arrived at the funeral home to pay their respects to my mother's memory, it became very clear to me what her life purpose was. The stories, the anecdotes, the tears, and the laughter - it all came together. Her legacy was staring right at me.

All around the visitation room, there was evidence of family, children, nurturing and mothering. There were families with young children. There were families with older children. There were young adults who had spent their early years of life with my mother being their preschool teacher, who had chosen to give their own children that same experience.

Many friends remembered my Mom listening to them during hard times. She had always been a person they could trust with their most painful secrets. There were family members who recalled very similar stories of calling my mom when they needed gentle guidance.

Ever since I can remember, we had kids in our home - ranging in ages from a few months to the teenage years. My mother loved kids and was a natural nurturer. She was passionate about helping children learn to read and write and strongly believed in sending them to kindergarten ready to learn. She also made sure that the basic needs of each child were met. They would be fed if they needed to be fed, or clothed if they needed to be clothed. And if their parents were struggling in any way, my Mom found a way to help them get the support they needed. She was all about *family*. And to many of these parents, my mother was a part of their family - and they were a part of hers.

My mom had become known as "the second mother" for so many children as they were nurtured in her loving care, whether it was in her home daycare business or just as a "kid in the neighborhood." For any child who walked through her door, she gave everything she had and then some.

It was very clear that my mother had been a mother to many and it was a life that made her happy.

Hearing all these stories, it made perfect sense to my family and me, that in lieu of flowers, we would choose a charity that embodied my mom's passion for children and families, and for early childhood education. That part felt easy. It was the right way to honor her legacy.

The hard part was realizing the void that she was leaving behind. You never fully know the power of one's *ripple effect* until they're gone.

I can say, without a shadow of a doubt, my Mom changed lives. Mothering was her life purpose. It was her legacy.

We ALL have a life purpose legacy. What's yours?

Take a look at your ripple and you'll see that it's already present.

Bio

Tina M. Games is the author of Journaling by the Moonlight: A Mother's Path to Self-Discovery (an interactive book with an accompanying deck of 54 journaling prompt cards). As a certified creativity coach and life purpose intuitive, she is the "Moonlight Muse" for mothers who want to tap into the "full moon within" and claim their authentic self, both personally and professionally.

Through her signature coaching programs, based on the phases of the moon, Tina gently guides women from darkness to light as they create an authentic vision filled with purpose, passion and creative expression. For more information about her work please visit: www.JournalingByTheMoonlight.com where you can receive her 12 best tips for journal writing.

Chapter 14

Stop Seeking Life Balance

By Sherrice Kirby

"Spirit will be found in pure presence, the creative fire, the taunting of desire, the orgasmic pulse, the stilled calm, the birthing of light, all movement, all breath, this body is sacredly divine." - Sherrice Kirby

Heat, sweat, breathe, flow, undulate, move with the rhythm of breath, feel the stretch, the ache, the pleasure. Sounds sexy, doesn't it? So sorry to tease you, but, this is not going to be an erotica tell all, it's just hot Vinyasa flow yoga. This is the journey that stretched my physical and conscious limits, laid me down on a mat, drenched me in sweat to bring me before the altar of Self for a serious conversation about intention and integrity.

The Defining Moment

Last year marked a stake in the sand in the shifting artistry of my life. Choosing to re-engage in my floundering yoga and meditation practice that had taken a six-year leave of absence in the wake of parenting, business and the designing of a fantastic new life as a family. Fantastic to be sure but let's get real… "frantically frenzied" would be a more honest description.

My family, businesses, dog, and all the responsibilities that I had consciously chosen, had me running at an adrenal-fatiguing pace that was not going to slow unless I chose to stop. I know what you are thinking… "how does a self-professed type A, high achieving, 'busy badge' wearing powerhouse, hustle until I reach that mythical 'good enough' internal state?" When does a recovering-perfectionist, self-help wielding, example-setting mother stop?"

She doesn't… but she can perform a miracle with a subtle shift in perspective. Here's my message… stop seeking life balance and start the creation of rhythm and flow.

Stop believing that if you do it all, get it done, get it right, please, and perform that you can prevent pain and discomfort from taking up residence in your life. We tend to tell ourselves many stories, especially when we nurse what is showing up as "drama" and fail to wean it out of our lives; in spite of its parasitic effect on all that we love and cherish. It is hard for truth and authenticity to compete with our imagination's tale of self-worthlessness. So I chose to lean into the pain, stretch into the practice, accept, learn and move on. It took a year of yoga, three powerful intentions and a consistent commitment to the expansiveness of my heart to give birth to the peace that is now sitting inside my soul.

The Journey

My life was whispering to me; a failed project, a few intense coaching sessions, a couple "come to Jesus" moments with people holding the funds. Oh, and did I mention that I had stopped wearing jeans, as an odd fleshy bulge appeared at my waist upon donning my favorite, old, faded blues. All these reasons were nudging me to stop, get present, reconnect with intention, focus and get back to the integrity of my own agenda.

My body was desperately saying, "Get back to the gym, get out for a walk, and leave your desk". My physical health and wellness had always come so easy but what was once easy and addictive; now just felt like something else on the "to do" list.

My body was not feeling like the well cared for home of my past. Over the last two years, I would often drive to the gym and sit in the parking lot where I responded to various emails. Upon completion, I would drive away, never having left my car.

I took my workout gear on road trips but it never saw any action. The hustle for the cash and recognition became recklessly misaligned from the "why" of the great life that I had been designing.

It was in one of these moments of feeling so frenetically driven that my soul finally spoke to me through an invitation to attend a yoga class from my best friend. *"The divine will speak to you through those you love when you refuse to listen to yourself".*

This was an opportunity to start over and get back on the horse that I had fallen off of and refused to mount again. This was going to hurt inside and out. This was not going to look how it had in the past. Six years, a baby, and the neglect of my overall fitness were showing up in all areas of my life. I was not going to be the elite athlete, hot chic, wonder woman in the room. My ego was going to have to check itself at the door. My soul was going to have to hold space for fear and worthiness to work through the new decade of my life.

Very well... let the surrender begin. There I was, at the studio, sitting in my car, looking for an excuse to drive away. This is how the self talk went, "Dammit, I have to pay for parking, I don't have change. Shit, the meter takes a credit card that excuse is gone. I forgot a towel. I will get really sweaty. I better go home and come back another day with a towel. Oh, that's right, they rent towels. I forgot a change of underwear for after. Since when do you care if you go commando? GET YOUR ASS IN THE STUDIO before it gets any bigger!"

So, I entered the studio, trepidation in tow, wondering if my suit of "I am so conscious armor" is impressing anyone. I hide in the corner up front so I can at least see myself in the mirror and not play comparison games with my old self. Everyone is quiet. I lay down in Savansana. Suddenly, I realize that I am all-alone with myself, my body, and someone else is running the show. I am in my body with an empty mind and all I have to do is follow the prompts of the beautiful voice of direction.

I am responsibility free. No one is asking me for anything. I just have to be in my body. REALLY, REALLY be in MY body. I am free to be in my pure presence where I can surrender to the light of my intentions and manifest the silence in my mind. My heart will open when my mind stops chatting.

I am breath. I am calm. I am the stillness and this is freedom. 90 minutes of sheer freedom. This realization of the bliss I had been denying myself quickly became a liaison I could not resist. My path was altered to map out the pure white space of my yoga practice while the rest of my life learned to reclaim the wellness that had been put aside for much too long.

Each class offered an opportunity to set an intention. This beautiful metaphor manifested itself into every fiber of my body that year. Days turned to months of embodying the same intention I set in class. Until that intention molded itself into my being and its practice became habitual as opposed to being forced, I was not going to stop.

Where there is focus, there is expansion. All of my innate skills, talents and integrity were needed to create the strategy within my lifestyle to stay committed to the practice.

The amazing gift was bringing the person in the yoga studio into the practice of my daily life. Creating stillness in my soul, being the calm breather in all situations and sharing the lightness of my heart with the world around me was my mission. This is still a practice that I tend to daily and I expect I always will.

Simple Intentions of Pure Transformation

These are the intentions and some questions that came to me over the course of the year. The amazing synchronicity is that the same questions were coming up in conversation with many of my client's during coaching sessions. There are no accidents. My yoga practice was as much for them as it was for myself. My work was coming *through me* as opposed to *from me*. And what I learned was there was a bigger reason for my practice than my own personal transformation.

Trust Yourself

- Why do you want what you want?
- Does your ego or soul desire this outcome?
- Who's vision are you fulfilling?
- What is at stake if you push on without stopping to search? What is at the seat of the desire?
- You are fully equipped with everything you need for this lifetime.
- Expand your heart and open your mind to the possibility that the

answer you seek is right in front of you. It is possibly the nudge or the butterfly or the slight feeling that what you are experiencing is something you have seen before.

- Is it really your voice that is screaming? If you stop listening to all the other voices, could you hear your own?
- Allow the soul, logic and intuition to dictate your readiness, instead of fear, ego or perceived authority

Let Go

- Allow life to flow through you, let go of all force.
- Let go of what is not of mutual contribution in this life.
- Create space for relationships that offer opportunity for service and support.
- Reframe, Reframe, and then Reframe again!
- The miracle is in the shift of perspective.

Gratitude for Everything Exactly How it IS!

- The wondrous journey that this life is taking you on.
- Every breath, every movement
- The nutrition and taste of your food
- The wonder in your daughter's eyes and the smell of her hair as her head is pressed against your chest.
- The pleasure you experience with your husband.
- The opportunity to serve and add value to all life that is placed in your path.
- The twists, turns, yeses, no's and all decisions that have lead to the exact moment in time and space that you now share with all life around you
- Your bodies ability to stretch, it's strength, and flexibility

- Your mind's ability to problem solve and consciously choose
- Freedom, Funds, and fun
- Creation, Connection, Contribution and Celebration

Integrity with Soul

Yoga is a practice as is life. There is no arrival point, just surrender to the journey. I will be honest here; accepting that I will not arrive is a challenge for someone with an innate ability and talent for driving results. I am finding there is a new consciousness to how I learn, grow and move to a space of integrity within my soul. The ability to choose perspective is proof that freedom is within our mind and soul!

My Intentional Desire for YOU

Try a yoga class or find a practice that takes you to a space of surrender within your body. Your mind and heart will thank you for the expression of freedom that an intentional journey will take you on. You deserve this and your body needs it. You are worth your healthiest and most joyous self!

Bio

Professionally Certified Executive Coach, Corporate Consultant, Business Development Specialist, and a thought leader in "the art of life design". Visionary, entrepreneur, writer, strategist, adviser, speaker, passionate creator of clarity, action and manifestor of results!

Sherrice's passion for a health, wellness and the pursuit of excellence has been a lifelong journey, as a competitive athlete, entrepreneur, personal coach and business consultant. Sherrice has 15+ years in multiple positions within sales, marketing, sales training, management and corporate consulting for Fortune 500 and private companies. Sherrice has created her own businesses, sold businesses, lead and produced seven figure business projects, consulted in multiple industries ranging from medical, finance, esthetic, personal training, personal development, event planning, the arts, editorial, athletics, government and more.

Sherrice's coaching style is honest, intuitive and very real; balancing a strong push for results with compassion and heart. Sherrice is a Yogi and Reiki Master; this work has helped to bring spirit to her strong corporate background.

Chapter 15

Learning to Live According to My Highest Values and Intuition

By Meghan Kerner

Today, I am so grateful to be exactly where I am… a mother to a beautiful daughter. All throughout my path, my number one method of decision-making is to follow my intuition. I am at peace knowing that the Universe will always take care of me and that I am in the perfect place at the perfect time, even if it does not always appear that way.

I am so grateful to have the ability to find peace, joy, and love within myself at any moment regardless of what is happening around me. However, my life was not always this way.

From the time I was young, I was encouraged to excel – in school, sports, and extracurricular activities. I was taught that girls can do anything that boys can do. I bought into that belief and not only wanted to be an equal with the guys, I wanted to beat them.

I went to an all-girls high school where I received the message that smart girls become doctors, lawyers, engineers, or go to business school. Only young women with bad grades went to art school or (heaven-forbid!) had children and became stay-at-home moms.

With these beliefs firmly in place, I went to college and got 2 degrees in engineering. But by the end of graduate school, my body was screaming out in pain that I was in the wrong place. Gratefully, I listened to my gut, left engineering, and decided to use my analytical skills and overachieving workaholic attitude in the business world.

When I turned 30, my biological clock started ticking quite loudly. I remembered one of my childhood dreams was to become "the best mom ever." At the time, I was working long hours for too little pay with a nightmare commute in Los Angeles traffic.

I knew that working for myself would give me more flexibility once I had kids. So, I quit my job to work on building a business full time in order to have something up and running before the baby came.

One of the first challenges I ran into was constantly judging myself and comparing myself to other business owners. After second guessing myself on a dozen different business ideas, I realized that the fastest and easiest way for me to actually make money was to offer my marketing skills to other business owners. So, I started working as a search engine optimization (SEO) consultant helping local business owners get to page 1 on Google.

I established an LLC and invested in my education to become better at selling and marketing. It seemed like I was always working and striving to improve, even though I had started my business to create more freedom and flexibility in my life. Since I was determined to "be successful" by the time I had a baby, I kept pushing myself to get more clients, increase revenue, and build a bigger business. After 2 years, I still wasn't satisfied that the business was "successful enough," even though I had never specified what that actually meant. And to add insult to injury, I was struggling with fertility challenges.

It was extremely painful to slow down and face the facts of what was really going on in my life at that time. But I had reached a breaking point. I was frustrated, exhausted, stressed, and overwhelmed. So I decided to slow down and really take a deeper look at was going on in my life. I saw that I was spending a majority of my time doing things that were not in alignment with my goal to start a family or my highest personal values of love, spiritual growth, and freedom. I saw that I continually pushed myself to do more, learn more, and earn more out of fear that if I didn't then I wouldn't be "good enough" or worthy of love from those around me. I saw that I started my business with the goal of making money as quickly as possible because I equated net worth with self worth.

After that painful, truthful, period of self-reflection, I decided to make some changes in my life. I realized that I need to live in alignment with what was most important to me. I chose to stop pushing myself to grow my business and instead let it evolve naturally.

To my surprise, it continued to grow at the same pace, even though I was no longer working nearly as much. I took a course to learn about how to embrace my feminine side — how to relax, play, create, and enjoy life more fully. It seems ridiculous to me now that I had to relearn those basic life skills but as a workaholic, it was absolutely necessary.

On the fertility side, I started to work with an osteopath and nutritionist to get my body ready to conceive. Both reminded me about the importance of letting go of any expectation of when I would get pregnant. I had to surrender to the fact that I couldn't control when it would happen. I could only prepare my body as best I as possible and let nature take its course.

A close friend also reminded me that as much as I wanted to start a family, I must always remember that having a baby does not guarantee happiness. Joy can only truly come from within one's self. So I focused on choosing to be a peace and letting go of my need to get pregnant as soon as possible. To my surprise, I conceived only 2 months after beginning to work with my new doctor and nutritionist!

It has taken me quite some time to remember that as a child I was a nurturing, creative, joyful soul. I loved to sing and dance as I walked through life and I naturally seemed to enjoy taking care of my younger sisters. Looking back I can see that somewhere along the way, I picked up the belief that while it was great to have those qualities they would not get me very far in the "real world."

It was as if my nurturing, creative, whimsical, feminine qualities were great to have but only as add-ons to a quality work ethic, discipline and perseverance to get things done without concern about personal cost. I do not know where I picked up these messages and I do not blame anyone for having that attitude. After all, it has led me to where I am today and it has been a hell of a journey.

In the past year, I delegated almost all of the ongoing operations in my business to allow me to take maternity leave. It was amazing to me that I had built my business in a way that made it possible to serve my clients with the same quality as always and have the time and energy needed to nurture a newborn.

I finally started writing about topics dear to my heart on my website LoveLightFreedom.com. I was so scared to let my SEO clients

and business colleagues find out that I have this spiritual side to me…
it seems so un-businesslike! But I knew that I couldn't wait any longer
to start encouraging other people to allow themselves to pursue what
truly matters: love, spiritual growth, and the freedom to live life as you
please.

So what are the takeaways that I'd like to share with you? Life
works in ways that I do not always understand. I have found that when
I make decisions based on what feels right in my heart even though I
might not know why I am I doing what I'm doing, it always turns out
to be for a positive reason. On the other hand, any time I have a made
a decision in the hopes to speed up results, just to make money, or in
hopes of becoming "better" from a prideful ego perspective then the
universe gives me challenges and lessons that are not very pleasant. I
know now that my contribution to the world must be aligned with
what is fun, joyful, easy, and what comes naturally for me or I will not
do it for very long.

I want to let go of anything that involves me trying to become
someone other than who I am. I want to let my inner light shine in a
way that encourages others to let their light shine too.

Do what you want to do! Do what feels good to you! By that I
mean do what is in alignment with who you are. If you love to sing
then sing in the shower, record new melodies into your cell phone, sing
as you walk down the street, at birthday parties, at bus stations – not
with the expectation that you will be rewarded for it but so you can
share your joy with the world.

When you focus on bringing more joy to the world just by
following your bliss, then you will attract great things into your life. So
do what you love and what comes naturally to you as much as possible;
you will refine your talent and you will serve the world in a bigger way
just by being you.

When you chase after "success" (aka money, status, fame) and are
following "a plan" just so you can make money, then you will likely feel
empty because your business and your actions are not aligned with
your soul. I have seen this in my own life many times.

How many times have you made a commitment to something and

shortly thereafter, when it started feeling bad, you continued to force yourself to do it? I've done this dozens of times but I am committed to never doing it again. I now choose to slow down and take the scenic route on my journey and to enjoy my life each day, rather than work like crazy with the hopes of being happy someday in the unknown future. I now remind myself that it is better to gracefully decommit than to force myself to do anything that no longer is in alignment with my intuition and my highest values. And in every painful or challenging situation, I do my best to remember to forgive myself.

Now is the time to forgive yourself too. For the money you spent on the degree you aren't using or the business that isn't working. For the relationship that failed. For the not-so-nice things you said to yourself in a moment of frustration yesterday. Life will continue to challenge you, and the only way to find peace is to accept what is and forgive yourself and the world for being different than you had hoped. It is time to start tuning in to your heart and your intuition. Let the pure spirit within you guide your decisions, both big and small. Doing so does not mean that you will never face a challenge again but it will allow you to find peace within yourself, knowing that you are on the right place on your journey.

So the next time you ask yourself what you should do with your life, take heart that you are in the perfect place on your journey. Wherever you are now leads to wherever you are going next. Remember, there is no job or business or relationship that will make you happy. True joy comes from within - regardless of what is happening at work, in your family, or in the world at large. Take some time to tune into your highest values and see if you are allowing yourself to live by those values. They are different for everyone and it can be challenging to live according to your own truth in the world of today. But it can be done. No matter what life throws your way.

May you have the courage to live in alignment with your highest values and intuition knowing this always lead to gratitude, peace, and joy within your heart.

Bio

Meghan Kerner is the owner of The Zelite Group, LLC, which provides business coaching and online reputation management services. She also writes about fulfillment and spirituality at http://www.love-lightfreedom.com.

Chapter 16

Answering the Call of Wild Wisdom

By Lea Bayles

Late in January 2012, I was visiting my daughter, grandson and son-in-law in Cape Cod. In the very early hours, one snowy morning, I woke suddenly to a torrent of words demanding to be written.

You know those times... you wake up in the night and you seem to be getting a Big Download from Beyond as your little sleeping body is jolted by an immense force asking to be birthed into this world.

Maybe, like me, you sometimes heed the call while other times just grumble as you try, with varying degrees of success, to go back to sleep.

This time the words were so exciting and fresh I had no desire to sleep. *Wild Wisdom is not city water. It has not been piped, managed, studied, treated, purified, fluoridated or chlorinated. Wild Wisdom is water you slurp right out of the icy stream melting from the glacier....*

Instantly, I was filled with enormous vitality and excitement. *Oh, yes! Thank you for blessing me with this! I'm your woman! Yes indeed, I want to help birth this!*

I sat up and madly wrote in my notebook or rather, the words madly wrote themselves through me.

The next day I went about my day happily immersed in grand-motherly joys of making a birthday cake, changing diapers, singing silly songs, reading Curious George and building alphabet block tower all the while, in the background of my awareness, there hummed the nourishing and fortifying vibrancy of the creative force, both mysterious and as familiar as my own hands. I looked forward to playing with the words, surrendering deeply to their intention and letting them have their way with me.

Then I lost it all. I looked through all my notebooks and could not find the words I had scribbled so fervently in the darkness.

Over the next few months, the needs of the world seemed to take up all of my creative energy. My father became increasingly ill and died in July. In those demanding months, I frequently thought of Wild Wisdom, and felt its intensity calling me, like a lover who is willing to wait for a while if he must, but will not be put off for long.

In September, I awoke again with Wild Wisdom streaming through my body and mind. Again, in the early hours I wrote and again was carried along by a rushing river of vitality. Surrendering to the presence of the words, I felt linked with a primal force of nature within myself.

I felt eager to share this writing with others. Then, predictably, terror and dread filled my being. Resistance was ready to strangle the voice of my own Wild Wisdom.

No more! After years of practice, I have become increasingly adept at transforming the polarity of fear into a dance of creative power that energizes. *Yes!* I say to Wild Wisdom, *Yes!*

At a magical Winter Solstice gathering in our barn studio, I first offered Wild Wisdom as a performance piece. Just as carloads of guests arrived, a sudden windstorm swept through, knocking out the electricity, leaving us to experience Wild Wisdom by flickering candlelight. It was a perfection we could not plan, but laughingly welcomed and savored.

Wild Wisdom is, by its very nature, a mysterious power, impossible to fully define. It cannot be controlled by human will, yet it is eager to partner with each of us.

Perhaps you also feel Wild Wisdom, in the rush of your blood and the marrow of your bones. You can feel it in your dreamscapes, in the trees and surf and in your fierce longings.

Join me in exploring the call of Wild Wisdom!

Wild Wisdom

Wild Wisdom is not city water.

It has not been piped, managed, studied,
treated, purified, fluoridated or chlorinated.
It does not pour obediently
out of your household fixtures.

Wild Wisdom does not stop when you turn a knob.
It does not travel around the world
encased in layers of plastic wrap.
It does not end up in the landfill or
kill baby albatross.

Wild Wisdom is water you slurp
right out of the icy stream melting off the glacier.
Wild Wisdom gushes from a
mysterious subterranean vein.
In it, you taste ancient minerals from
plant and animal bodies
decomposed nine million years ago.

Wild Wisdom flows through the cave where your
bushmothers gathered and ate aurochs and
painted with their hands and worshipped
fecundity, food, survival and spirit.

Wild Wisdom is not the pet on your leash.
It is the untamable creature who claims you as kin,
quickening your pulse,
breathing your breath,
seizing your senses.
Leopard, sea anemone, dragonfly,
languid bear sleeping with cubs,
fox staring boldly in the forest,
dying rabbit,
lion stalking,
roebuck running,
serpent wrapped close around your warm belly,
raven offering you a courtship rattle,
amber eyes shining in the night.

Wild Wisdom is not a Wal-Mart tomato.
It has not been manipulated to stay pretty

on the shelf for months.
It has not been gassed and shipped from a
hot dry field in Mexico to Nebraska in January.

Wild Wisdom is a lumpy, funky, weird,
reddish-brown tomato
that alerts your tongue to
new possibilities of delight.

Wild Wisdom is the soles of your feet
longing for bare earth,
longing to grow roots that
descend and spread,
longing to seek nourishment
among the thick, gnarly organs and
fragile filaments of
oak, yew, fir, alder, cedar and redwood,
longing to rise as sap up and up and up and
out to offer leafside to sun,
longing to reunite with the Tall Ones who
towered above for centuries and
whose presence beckons you still through
strip malls, subdivisions and tree farms.

Wild Wisdom does not have a marketing plan.
It does not work 9-5 and take two weeks vacation.
It is not in the voter's pamphlet.

It does not rule from a throne or a boardroom or a pulpit.
It does not tell you to follow rules that it violates.

Wild Wisdom is not a polite guest.
She crashes the party and seduces the host,
eats with his fingers from other peoples' plates,
belches loudly, dances on the table and
spills red wine all over your precious manuscript.

Wild Wisdom is in you.
It needs you.
And god knows …you need it.
You need it to come alive.
You need it to find your path.
You need it to stay true to your core.

You need it to grow into your

honest version of lover, friend, mother, father,
teacher, artist and healer,
instead of the pale imitation who has for years
gotten you such nice nods of approval.

Wild Wisdom may shatter the container,
to save the contents.

Wild Wisdom shakes up your marriage
so you both have a chance to discover
what you really came together to create.
Wild Wisdom wakes you up at 2 in the morning and,
yes, you can ignore her,
I tried for years,
so go right ahead and
pathologize her as a sleep disorder,
do an herbal protocol for your liver or
get a prescription for Ambien
to try to make her leave you alone or
-Good Grief!- at least
come back at a civilized hour!

But honey, do you really want her to leave you alone?
Are you sure?

Wild Wisdom is the potency of the eggs you will not shed,
eggs that become memes for our new story,
fertilized and brought to life as
you make love with your creative destiny.

Wild Wisdom is always cooking deep
in the warm darkness of your loins,
ready to impregnate possibilities
we have barely begun to dream of.

Wild Wisdom is the 13th Godmother not invited to the christening,
Lilith banished from the Garden,
Holy Infant dumped in a trashcan,
Aphrodite locked out of the wedding chamber,
Greenman starving in your basement,
Brilliant Poet forgotten in the asylum.

Wild Wisdom is the shaman who
strengthens your spine as you
bear witness to the horror of

mountains beheaded, forests demolished,
oceans acidified and children starving.

He is the trickster who
cracks you open to love beyond human reason,
gives you courage to take a stand,
shoves you off your comfort ledge and
clashes a terrible gong just when
you've reached enlightenment.

He is the Timber Wolf who chews off his leg to be free.

Wild Wisdom may shine through in
your biggest mistake, a failed career,
the time you didn't meet your responsibilities,
gave up and disappointed everyone.

Wild Wisdom may summon you to
turn down the generous donor,
gorgeous lover and ideal job.

Wild Wisdom may show up in the
cancelled meeting, dead battery,
prime opportunity snatched away....

Making room for something new.

Each day, dear one, you get to choose.
Curse him?
Or embrace him as ally?

Wild Wisdom is coming in through the cracks and
under our doors and through our dreams.
She hisses and cackles out of withered lips and
touches the world with just born fingers.

Wild Wisdom is here to save you and to
save everything you most cherish.
Wild Wisdom knows we cannot
open to the fullness of our longing,
cannot serve our sweet planet and cannot
evolve into our next stage of being human,
without her.

Wild Wisdom is not the words

you practice and edit until they are perfect.
It is the vapor that rises at the very
edge of what you know,
tantalizing your palate with ideas you
do not fully grasp.

Your Wild Wisdom may need
chaotic drumming and drooling dancing to
set it free.

Your Wild Wisdom may need
people who hold tender space,
giving lavish permission to be timid,
ridiculous, clumsy, too quiet and too loud
as you become a conduit for the voice that has
not yet found its way into this world.

Wild Wisdom needs you to stop hiding behind:
I don't know. I'm not enough. I'm not ready.
And to start saying, *Hell yes, I'll give it a try!*

Wild Wisdom needs you to stop trying to figure it all out
and to be done with bowing to authority.

Wild Wisdom is light in trees,
frogs singing,
bright moon in the early morning sky,
books dropping off the shelf,
valiantly flirting with you to help you wake up.

Resistance is suffering.

How many more times?
How many more times will you
ignore, medicate, placate, distrust,
second guess, tune-out and over-ride
your Wild Wisdom?

Wild Wisdom may give up on you and
crawl into a tight corner of a dark closet.
Listen.
Can you hear him crooning softly back in the shadows?
Sit quietly.
Wait to see if he is willing to come out again to talk to you.

My beloved friend,
What if she – in you –
he- in you-
has the piece of our puzzle…
the elixir for our healing…
the vision of our emerging world…
that only you
— *only you* — can deliver?

Wild Wisdom is calling.

Will you answer?

Bio

Lea Bayles, MA, helps soulful, smart women transform struggle into ease, fear into creative vitality and confusion into clarity as they become their most loving, glorious and world-changing selves. Lea's playful, practical, compassionate and mystical approach draws from her master's degree in psychology and experience with theater, dance, mind-body healing, energy work, yoga, tantra and chi-kung and her personal challenges and joys with living in a body. She has created the *Co-Creating Heaven on Earth* interviews with visionaries, *Replenish Your Soul* meditation series, numerous articles and integrative wellness curricula and the popular guidebook, *Take Back Your Life: Moving from Chronic Pain to Lifelong Healing* and is a masterful facilitator, speaker, teacher, healer and coach.

Please visit www.LeaBayles.com for your inspiring free audio recording and video of *Wild Wisdom* and to receive the weekly, *Creative Flow in Five*, playful, potent, life-changing practices and tips. Activate your river of vitality, creativity, joy and delight…in less than five minutes!

Chapter 17

The Journey to Fulfillment

By Shari Beaudette

"What's fulfillment," my 8 year old asked me when I explained what I was writing. "Hmm. Good question," I told him, and started to explain. But he was gone. Quickly distracted by our 6-year-old daughter calling from the next room for someone to please help with the iPad... aka the distraction machine.

I was left standing alone. Cycling back and forth, once again, between my children's reality and my own childhood. Past wounds scratching at my consciousness - even after 32 years of healing.

And I realized that my son's question was the nugget of inspiration I needed or rather it was his ability to ask a question... without really needing an answer.

That is what fulfillment is for me.

It is being able to ask these kinds of questions. And having the tools, space and freedom to embrace a lifelong journey of personal growth. It's hope and optimism. It's being able to pause and reflect on what's important to me and why and then taking action to live in alignment with my values. It's about finding the gifts and lessons in each moment. It's learning to release the parts of my story (childhood trauma and unintentional neglect) that no longer serve me. It's learning to write my own story. And it's about serving from a place of empathy, gratitude, love and wisdom and to make a positive difference in the lives of others.

My journey to fulfillment is just that - a journey. It has more twists and turns than I ever could have imagined in my nearly 40 years.

I was born in the early 70's to a mother who never stood a chance. Her own childhood abuse, neglect and trauma left her inadequately equipped. Her past, coupled with postpartum depression, were enough to send her off the deep end forever. I know she tried at least once to take her own life. Her diagnosis had vacillated between bipolar and schizophrenia.

Somehow, she kept us in her less-than-stable custody until I was nearly 8. Then, our father was able to get custody of us. She has been institutionalized for 30+ years now and incapable of emotion, relationships or reality.

I share this because I know we all have our stories. Part of finding fulfillment is knowing and acknowledging your story and then finding a way to "mine" for the gifts and lessons. It is about learning to release what no longer serves you.

What are my gifts? Resilience, independence, intuition and empathy. I learned to embrace change and re-frame challenges. To make the best of things and to keep the peace. I just wanted everyone to be happy. I think my love and craving of personal development, wellness and proactive self-care - were all born from seeing what happened to my mother, from a lack of stability and of course, wondering how much of it was preventable.

I cannot say that I had the clarity or wherewithal to notice all of this in my youth. I actually thought I coped just fine. I did well in school, earned my Bachelors in Exercise and Sport Science and then a Masters in Business Administration. I traveled the world, ran a full marathon and bought my first home. I got married, settled down and then the journey into motherhood began which rocked my world.

I had endured some postpartum complications with our firstborn in 2004 and then two subsequent miscarriages thereafter. I faced major complications with my 4th pregnancy and was on bed rest for 100+ days (2 months actually in the hospital while my 2 year old was at home). Our daughter was born 8 weeks early and diagnosed with a rare lung disease that she thankfully outgrew after 10 months.

I struggled to hold it all together during these years and completely lost the strong, growth oriented, resilient woman I thought I was. I was stuck in survival mode, just going through the motions. I was triggered left and right as the pressure on me caused all the old wounds to come back. I cried a lot of "poor me."

I was watching all sorts of junk on TV trying to escape the reality of being overwhelmed with fear. I felt so ill equipped to be a good mother. I had no idea how to be one. I was exhausted, overextended and miserable. I remember talking to a group of friends, "Oh, I used to love personal development and self-growth but now I'm a lost cause. At this point, it's better to escape reality," Everyone laughed. Everyone understood.

Well, I did not like the way it was. I was NOT going to sit back and do nothing. Frankly, I had already overcome and achieved so much in my life that I was not okay with "just surviving." I also realized that I was not being the role model I wanted to be for my children. I wanted to thrive and help others do the same.

So how *do* you find fulfillment? Embrace the SPA Time Living movement: Self-care Promotes Ability.

"S" in SPA can stand for… systematizing self-care or stress management or spirituality. Reconnect to your higher power. Slow down and tune into what you need. Take the time to determine what self-care actually means to you. For me, self-care is about staying connected to my values and purpose through meaningful work, mediation, mindfulness and movement. Yoga has been a big part of the movement component and learning to build habits and rituals around these practices has changed my life.

The "P" in SPA can stand for: Purpose, passions, productivity, priorities or protecting boundaries. We must remove ourselves from messages of negativity and unfulfilled desires - or at least learn to regularly cleanse this constant chaos coming at us. Purpose is a significant source of energy, strength and fulfillment found within. Fulfillment occurs when we shift from focusing on our shortfalls to reconnecting with our deep sense of purpose, values and passions. It is about knowing our deepest selves. Only then can we move forward and "be productive" in the areas that actually matter to us and make a difference.

The "A" can stand for: Authenticity, action, accountability and awareness. Seek your true self. Let your actions flow from a place of deep self-knowing. Fulfillment takes place when we are most authentic and real with ourselves. I know all too well what happens when we try to live into everyone else's shoulds and shouldn'ts. For me, I so desperately wanted to be a good mother. I was constantly judging and comparing myself at every turn. I was sacrificing everything that made me whole. It all backfired. I missed the critical step of "refilling my own tank. "

The infamous oxygen mask expression, *"you must put your own oxygen mask on first before you put your children's or others on"* became far too intertwined in our lives. It took several lessons for me to get the message: my partial collapsed lung caused me extreme pain because I was not breathing fully after my firstborn was my first real clue. Learning to live with an oxygen tank for our second baby for 10 months and her rare lung disease helped me to finally get the message. Never forget the value of deep breathing… especially through pain. I have chimes and reminders built into my day, my life and work. For me, my family and my clients.

How about you? Are you protecting, nurturing and cultivating your ability? Have you built in habits of regular renewal and self-care?

Grab a pen and paper and here's a quick exercise to kick-start for mindful, conscious, spa time living… right now!

Physical

• Jot down 3+ ways that energize, renew or support you physically. Think deep breathing, meditation, exercise, water, healthy eating. Grab your calendar and schedule in at least one small act from #1 EVERY DAY. Yes really.

• Write down 3+ things that seem to function as holes in your physical energy pool. Pause and breathe… tuning into what you might need to change or release. Set the intention to take action and release, reframe or reassess.

Emotional

• Jot down 3+ ways that energize, renew or support you emotionally. Think: asking for help, helping others, connecting with kindred spirits. Grab your calendar and schedule in at least one small act from #1 EVERY DAY. Yes really.

• Write down 3+ things that seem to function as holes in your emotional energy pool. Pause and breathe… tuning into what you might need to change or release. Set the intention to take action and release, reframe or reassess.

Intellectual

• Jot down 3+ ways that energize, renew or support you intellectually. Think: learning, growing, completing tasks. Grab your calendar and schedule in at least one small act from #1 EVERY DAY. Yes really.

• Write down 3 + things that seem to drain you intellectually. Pause and breathe… tuning into what you might need to change or release. Set the intention to take action and release, reframe or reassess.

Spiritual

• Jot down 3+ ways that energize, renew or support you spiritually. What I mean by spiritual is connecting to your deep seated values and higher self. Think: prayer, meditation, nature, solitude, meaningful/purposeful work. Grab your calendar and schedule in at least one small act from #1 EVERY DAY. Yes really.

• Write down 3+things that seem to function as holes in your energy pool. Pause and breathe… tuning into what you might need to change or release. Set the intention to take action and release, reframe or reassess.

Bio

Shari Beaudette, founder of SpaTimeLiving.com, helps busy women stay happy and healthy through the Art of Guilt-free Non-negotiable Self-care. With a BS in Exercise and Sport Science, MBA in Organizational Development and 200hr yoga teacher training, Shari is also a spa aficionado, creator of Chaos Cleanse™ Virtual Programs, and author of the forthcoming book, *Life Lessons Learned from Laundry: 10 Mindful Living Habits to Cleanse the Chaos when Work, Life and Laundry Keep Piling Up.*

Chapter 18

Women, Business & God

By Kelly O'Neil

"The world will be saved by the Western woman."
- Dalai Lama, Vancouver Peace Summit

For years, I have told my clients, "Everything you truly desire is on the other side of fear. You can experience fear or you can experience faith… it is your choice. For real lasting change to happen you must be willing to get comfortable with being uncomfortable. You have to have faith that everything will turn out for your higher good because that is how the universe works." And this advice is… well… uncomfortable. And it is 100% true.

It's important that they understand this because the women I work with (and a few very special men) are game changers – some on an international level and some in their communities and families. They have big visions, big hearts and a desire to do meaningful work and impact the world. And just like me, their spiritual connection is an important part of who they are. Call it God, Universe, The One, Source Energy, Higher Power or whatever your word is for it, they hold a belief in a power operating in the universe that is greater than oneself. This word provides a sense of interconnectedness with all living creatures, and an awareness of the purpose and meaning of life that helps them find meaning, hope, comfort, and inner peace in their life.

However, like many spiritual seekers (and up until the last few years I would include myself in this), the trend I see is that human beings started exploring spirituality because they want to "get" something. Something they felt they didn't already have. They want to attract more money into their business or find their ideal mate or live in a bigger house - a phenomenon that was kicked off by the movie "The Secret". And what I find when speaking with them is that they LOVE the idea of the Law of Attraction – I mean, who wouldn't want to attract more love, more money, more life, more of anything you want into your life – just so long as they don't have to walk through the discomfort to get it. That is where they get stuck.

It is natural as human beings to avoid (sometimes at all costs) feeling uncomfortable. We resist, push back, and procrastinate. We become cranky, we oversleep, overeat, overdrink and if we can afford it, overspend. The list of self-abuses just goes on and on. And we do all of this unconsciously, not even realizing that these actions are doing absolutely nothing to service our personal growth, our purpose and our tribes.

And I get it: change is uncomfortable. Feeling comfortable comes from knowing what to expect, maintaining a status quo and staying within our same old boundaries and belief systems. In order to make a lasting change, we have to shift our paradigms and tear down those walls that have been keeping us so "safe" all those years, climb beyond our self-imposed terror barriers and allow the Big Breakdown to happen.

You know, as well as I do, The Big Breakdown? It's what comes before The Big Breakthrough. The Big Breakdown is the uncomfortable period where the transformation starts to take place. It comes through painful thoughts like, "Who do you think you are to believe this or think you can do that?" Technology goes haywire, like computers crashing and dead Internet lines and cell phones that magically no longer work. Often money challenges come up (it's all energy right?) like unexpected bills or clients who can't pay or failed business projects. At times there are physical manifestations in our bodies like the flu or aches and pains or chronic inexplicable conditions. And for no real good reason we feel angry, frustrated and scared so we fall back on behavior patterns like procrastination or avoiding over commitment when we know; deep down, that it would serve us best to face our fears and discomfort head on. But our sneaky little egos try to use all this information to stop us... "See... you were going to fail anyway. Turn back. Come back to safety. Abort Mission! Abort Mission!"

If you have the conscious awareness to see this and you are supported in a way that aligns you more with faith than fear then you can stay connected long enough to see that all of this discomfort is actually a very good thing! Because just beyond The Big Breakdown and The Terror Barrier is The Big Breakthrough where you'll find everything you want and need to grow, succeed and manifest all that you truly desire in service of living your life purpose. Actually, everything you have ever needed, you have always had. The Big Breakdown is the Universe's way of getting us to step back and see it. Our initial reaction to The Big Breakdown is to abandon ship and sprint to safety. I've been there and I totally get it and it kept me stuck for years. However, when I learned to align myself more with faith than fear and I taught myself to be comfortable with the uncomfortable, I felt a sense of peace knowing that right past The Big Breakdown is The Big Breakthrough... and that's where the all the magic happens.

My lesson began in the early summer of 2010. I was in my home office in my 2.5 million dollar tear-down home that we could barely afford, nestled in the foothills of the affluent community I had been born and raised in. It was gorgeous outside and while my puppies lay snuggled up peacefully at the foot of my desk in their designer puppy bed, my world was falling apart... fast.

2009 was a dream year for me. As a motivational speaker, best-selling author and award winning brand-marketing coach, things couldn't have been better. I just had my large live workshop and sold out both levels of my high-end coaching program in less than 3 days pushing my company to the 7 figure level. I was highly sought out as a marketing expert to attract affluent clients and coach high performing entrepreneurs and I was being pursued by the top names in the industry for book deals and speaking appearances. As a reward, I had bought myself and my assistant BMWs for all our hard work and took my team on an all-expense paid trip to The Sonoma Mission Inn in Napa for spa treatments and wine tasting. I had finally arrived. *Or so I thought.*

I had worked extremely hard to make a name of myself and create extraordinary financial success. My clients were my family and I was beyond committed to doing whatever it took to provide them with an extraordinary experience that was transformational for their business and their life – even at the expense of mine. There was no "Me". I was defined by my business and my bank account and creating a 7 figure business was all consuming. I was becoming a workaholic even at the expense of my marriage, my friendships and my health. Even as I was teetering the scales at 263 pounds and suffering from anxiety and adrenal burnout caused by prolonged stress, I finally felt like I was someone who mattered in the world - a feeling I had been after for over 35 years. And I was quickly developing the inflated ego to prove it.

The euphoria of my sweet victory didn't seem to last long. By late January of 2010, messages that I was swiftly veering off path were hurdling at my head like bricks from the big guy upstairs. I had created a joint venture partnership with a "GURU" in our industry who turned out to be more sizzle than steak and abandoned our project midstream leaving me cash tight and scrambling for a new strategic plan. I had over-invested in the business (the kind of investment that could buy you a house in most places) and a very high-end coach that I had chosen for ALL the wrong reasons and was scrambling to make ends meet on my obscene monthly financial commitments. While the majority of my perfect high-end coaching group was sailing along making huge strides and big financial increases in their business, a couple of the members began to act out, wouldn't do the work, didn't like the group and started to make our team's life miserable.

Over the course of the spring, while opportunities piled in for media, speaking and joint venture engagements, I saw additional signs of trouble lurking.

Having been raised in a dysfunctional home with an alcoholic mother and a verbally and emotionally abusive father, I seemed to always have a special talent for attracting wolves in sheep's clothing into my life and my business. It was as if I was running around with a special sign on my forehead that said "Open for Abuse… Apply Within" that was only visible to people that had bad intentions. And while I had done years of personal development work and therapy, my wounds ran deep and were safely hidden behind size 22 pants.

At this point, my private coaching practice had sold out and I was only serving VIP clients. While 99% of the VIP clients were amazing entrepreneurs with big hearts and big dreams who went on to create stellar success, it was the 1% that took me down.

After publicly singing my praises for over 6 months, "Amy" ran into financial issues after failing to implement the plan developed for her. She began to ask for free advice and coaching and at first, I obliged. At that point in my life, clear boundaries were never really on my radar and I was a consistent over-giver. I just wanted everyone to be happy and everyone to love me. But after a few months of the same conversation, I finally got up the courage and told her that if she wanted to continue coaching with me she would have to sign a new contract. She didn't have the money and that is when the situation turned for the worse.

Amy began to harass me and my office staff on email and the phone. When that strategy wasn't effective, she asked me for a refund saying that I hadn't delivered what I promised. After the extensive work I had done combined with all the extra complimentary coaching and my unrelenting encouragement for her to implement what we had spoken about, a refund was not an option. This refusal is what pushed her off the deep end. Within a few short weeks she had threatened the lives of me and my family, wrote terrible lies about me on the internet, contacted all of the people on my fan page personally, contacted all the conferences that booked me to speak and filed complaints against me with any agency in the state of California who would allow it. And then she attempted to sue me. I was devastated.

Her erratic behavior was making me very nervous… actually I was scared because I had no idea what she would do next. I ended up filing a police report and requesting a restraining order. When we ended up in court, the judge tossed the case in 5 minutes as her claim was fraudulent and ordered her to stop harassing me.

Here and there, I will see her assume another pen name and write something unkind about me, but in large part, it stopped. As it later turned out, I learned this was a habit of hers when I was subpoenaed to testify against a victim she had sunk her teeth into after me.

I had been very distracted by this entire debacle but I still had clients who needed me and a team that was depending on me. I was committed to get my eye back on the ball until the next brick smacked me in the head.

We had an unhappy woman in my mastermind program who was facing her terror barrier and I lacked the leadership skills to deal with the issue and frankly I was exhausted from dealing with the last challenge. So I ignored it, until I had no choice but to deal with it when she gathered a small group of the group together and they staged a rebellion. I was devastated.

I learned pretty quickly that I wasn't the only high level coach that this had happened to but that was of little solace to me as everything I had worked so hard for the past two years was blowing up in my face.

My ego was having a holy fit about it as I sat there in my office chair with an overwhelming feeling of nausea, anxiety, anger and disbelief. Tears started pouring down my cheeks and I began to sob. My husband came into the office and asked me what was going on and all I could reply was "What do you do when your absolute best isn't good enough?"

And this was the beginning of my major Nervous Breakthrough. *(AKA The Big Break Down Before The Big Breakthrough.)*

> "Ruin is a gift. Ruin is the road to transformation." '
> - Elizabeth Gilbert

After nearly a decade of doing the work I was absolutely passionate about and had dedicated my life to and by most accounts was very gifted at, I had never felt more lost. Even in the midst of the crisis, I had remained conscious enough and had coached enough people through experiences like this to ask myself the defining question: For What Purpose Had I Attracted This Experience Into My Life? I knew that the universe (I wasn't quite ready to call it God at that point) always provided you experience to help you become more of who you really are. So I sat quietly in my office and I began to pray for the answer. What am I to learn here? Please guide me.

The answer came unexpectedly. As I sat unsure of what to do with myself, aside from pray, and ask myself the same question over and over again, out of the corner of my eye I saw a book a friend had given me about a spiritual retreat program she attended. I had this overwhelming sense that I had to do whatever it took to get there. And my intuition was correct.

After years of seeking to make the deep pain of my childhood wounds stop (some healthy ways– therapy, Catholic Church, Alanon, self-help books – and some not so healthy ways – over eating, over working, over spending, over drinking and over loving) it was in a remote cabin in the woods of St. Helena in less than 10 days that I found my way home… to myself.

While I had studied "spirituality", read the books a spiritual person is "supposed" to read, and watched the movie *The Secret* a hundred times, this spiritual center actually shifted my paradigm around spirituality and my relationship to God. Their practice supported me in loving myself and getting a better understanding of who I *really* am, who I am not and a way to heal the wounds of my past. They helped me to allow myself to live peacefully and on purpose in a way that serves the world. I will also share with you that living spiritually connected this way has also brought all of those things I desire into my life.

The awakenings of that spiritual retreat were endless. I learned that I had absolutely no idea who I really was. I had invented a brand that served its purpose to protect me from the outside world as I morphed to be the kind of person that could receive the love from whoever was in front of me – family, clients, peers, mentors, and friends. I had become a master chameleon and didn't even know I was doing it. I was addicted to people's approval of me and was behaving extremely co-dependently, which is very common of adult children of alcoholics. I had no healthy boundaries, I gave my power away constantly and I consistently invited abusers into my life because at some deep core level, I believed that was all my I really deserved in life. I learned that I was hiding all of this behind a persona of a highly successful, got-it-all-together, powerhouse who talked a good game. At best I was surviving and even that was starting to crumble.

When I left the retreat, things began to instantly shift for me. I was now seeing the world in a different way. I had new tools to deal with life in a healthy way that allowed me in any moment to find my way home to myself. It was then that life began for me.

"Sometimes good things fall apart so better things can fall together."
- Marilyn Monroe

When I had arrived home from the retreat, life no longer reflected the woman I was becoming. I removed the personalized license plate from my luxury car. I transformed my office from a celebrity shrine filled with recognition to myself into a room that felt more like a luxury spa for meditation in my daily spiritual practice.

I committed to my health and began eating organic foods that would fill my body with the nutrients I needed to thrive and found a yoga studio that infused spirituality deeply into every class. Over the course of the next 18 months, I lost a little over 100 pounds and have never been in better shape.

I eliminated several toxic relationships from my life and came to the very hard decision with my husband to end our 6 year marriage. He is a wonderful guy... just not *my* guy. And we were able to end our marriage with love and dignity and respect and are still the best of friends today.

I made the decision to move out of the very comfortable hometown I had been born into and lived in for my entire life, to start a new adventure in a new city... all by myself.

And through my consistent meditation practice and work with my spiritual teachers and healers, I have gotten clearer about who I am, who I am not, what my life purpose is, what my mission is on this planet, and what is really important to me. And best of all, I found my unique voice. The one that was stifled as a little girl. Now, I am no longer afraid to use it. In fact, I believe it is the way in which I am meant to serve the world.

"Humanity is now faced with a stark choice: Evolve or die...
If the structures of the human mind remain unchanged,
we will always end up re-creating the same world, the same evils,
the same dysfunction."
- Eckhart Tolle

It is through my spiritual practice that I have come to believe the following:

- I believe we are all spiritual beings having a human experience. We return to earth and take a body with the express intention of evolving our level of consciousness by getting wounded, healing our wounds, discovering our individual life's purpose, serving our mission and ultimately to evolve our consciousness until we become "enlightened" (this could take many life cycles) and merge with "God" and relieve ourselves of the birth/life/death cycle.

- I believe that each of our lives is the expression of our reason for being.

- I believe that in the process of our human experience life provides us with consistent opportunities to evolve our level of consciousness. (Eckhart Tolle).

- And that every circumstance (as devastating, heartbreaking or painful as they may be) is happening FOR YOU and your greater good, not to you, in exactly the right time for you to evolve and serve your mission in the most impactful way.

Bio

After a successful corporate career as a brand strategist and publicist, Kelly O'Neil retired form corporate America in her late twenties and began her entrepreneurial journey. After amassing hundreds of thousands of dollars in debt and nearly going bankrupt, Kelly identified the strategies to create high six and seven figure success while doing work in the world that matters. Today, she is one of the most sought-after international brand marketing and leadership coaches for conscious entrepreneurs and aspiring women leaders who want to create Spiritually Rich™ businesses and embrace their inner leader.

Kelly is the winner of numerous awards including Top 50 Coolest Marketers (2009-2012), Be The Change celebrating women making a difference in the world and Seth Godin's "Purple Cow Award" naming Kelly's company as one of the most innovative companies in America. Kelly has given thousands of media interviews to outlets that include The Wall Street Journal, CNN, Bloomberg, Associated Press, The New York Times, USA Today, Time, Business Week, Forbes, Fortune, and even MTV. She also appears regularly as a speaker at professional associations, as well as national and international conferences and has consistently shared the stage with industry icons. She is the best-selling author of two books, "Visionary Women Inspiring the World: 12 Paths to Personal Power" and "Ignite Your Business Transform Your World." Her company, Kelly O'Neil International provides training, coaching and resources to women and entrepreneurs around the world.

Chapter 19

Making the Connection to Spiritual Fulfillment

By Lisa Vanderkwaak

"The true heart of relationships is connection. Deep, meaningful relationships are built by developing authentic connections with one another that recognize, inspire and nurture our unique spirits."
— Dr. Joseph Umidi

"That's it, I don't need them. I can live without them," I decided this when I was fifteen years old. Feeling hurt and rejected by family members led me to make this choice. The very people who were supposed to protect and care for me were refusing to support me when I needed it the most. It was then that I subconsciously decided to close off my heart, trust only myself, and prove that I could make it without others. You may be wondering how that worked out for me. Not very well. In fact, I discovered that the love and relationships I tried to push away were the very things I needed the most. The walls I put up in my heart to protect me from getting hurt did not draw a distinction between receiving love and avoiding pain. It kept everything out.

Perhaps you are like most people and can recall instances in your past where you felt disconnected rather than connected. If you were hurt too many times you may have believed that it was safer to close down part of your heart and not "feel" anymore. The discomfort of disconnection often leads people to seek out ways to numb the pain just to survive. If this is true for you I want to ask you: "What is the cost emotionally, relationally and spiritually?"

Brené Brown, a social worker and researcher set out to understand more about the relationship between human connection and shame.

Little did she expect that after six years of collecting data, her research findings would lead her to experience a "spiritual awakening". Her discoveries led to breakthroughs not only in her field of study, but also in her own life as they challenged her cognitive approach. During one of her TED talks called, *The Power of Vulnerability*, Brown confessed that her research led her down a path where she re-discovered who she really was and changed forever how she approached life, love and work. Her research findings indicated that it is within the context of connection that life becomes more fulfilling. She suggested that if you want to live wholeheartedly and more fulfilled, you need to be willing to engage in heart-centered connections. She went on to conclude that, "Connection is why we are here. It is what gives purpose and meaning to our lives."

As it was with me and with Brown, spiritual development may have begun in your life when you least expected it. In fact, if you are like most people, pursuing spiritual fulfillment may not be on the top of your list of priorities. Yet what I have discovered is that cultivating spiritual maturity is one of the essential keys to experiencing a richer, more fulfilling life and is a process that continues throughout your lifetime.

The process starts with an awareness that there is something missing in your life and continues as you intentionally cultivate relationships that engages your heart. What happens in the process is preparation for what lies ahead.

Along the spiritual journey, your self-awareness will become heightened and your heart will start to expand to contain more love than you ever thought possible. In fact, you will be challenged and become stretched in three main areas that also serve as indicators to your spiritual development.

These indicators show up in how you engage your heart, embrace the process of change, and how you express your uniqueness.

Engaging Your Heart

In his book, *Deadly Emotions*, Dr. Don Colbert shows the connection between illness and a person's emotional condition. He describes differences in how the brain and the heart operate. Colbert says that, "when the brain remains in the driver's seat, the heart – the soul, the seat of the emotions – can be abused, wounded, exploited, and end up filled with hurt and pain. A heart that is filled with pain is a heart that is stressed, and often depressed."

Even though the heart is the most powerful muscle in the human body, it can be severely strained by the pressures of the brain. Whenever we dismiss what our heart is trying to communicate and listen only to our mind, we suffer the dangerous consequences of what Paul Pearsall called "neglected heart syndrome." This in turn can lead to negative patterns of abuse, deprivation, and exploitation of the most sensitive part of who you are. Colbert concluded that tuning into your own heart allows you to experience the child within you which is the most sensitive part of your being, and which has the ability to awaken you to the joy of living.

In his book *Waking the Dead*, author John Eldredge said "To remain present to God, you must remain present to your heart. To hear His voice, you must listen with your heart. To love Him, you must love with all your heart. You cannot be the person God meant you to be and you cannot live the life He meant you to live, unless you live from the heart."

Will you set aside time today to listen to your own heart and get in touch with your spiritual core?

Embracing the Process

In the opening verse of Natalie Grant's song *In Better Hands* are the words "You can't be free if you don't reach for help. It's hard to love when you don't love yourself." This is a spiritual concept that highlights the importance of attending to the things of your own heart. You cannot properly love others if you do not love yourself. The law of life is summarized in this way: "Love God with your whole heart and love your neighbor *as yourself*."

This passage is not talking about some narcissistic way of living, expecting others to adjust to you. It refers to a healthy awareness of the greatness that lives inside of you and the value you possess because you are uniquely designed. You are a masterpiece created by the greatest artist of all time! As you learn to reconnect with your own heart, you will get in touch with: The way God wired you, how He intended for you to function and the purpose you are meant to fulfill. Loving yourself is based in a healthy acceptance of who you are at your core and that your value and worth are unchangeable no matter what has happened in your life. It is realizing you *do not need* to compete to be better than anyone or show anyone up, nor do you have to prove your worth. Instead, simply embrace who you are meant to be, with your strengths, gifts, and unique personality.

During my teenage years, my heart was highly charged with fears and bitterness. My environment was filled with constant chaos, destruction and confusion. By the time I was fifteen years old, I had rejected certain aspects of my family heritage that I had judged to be shameful and unacceptable. However, in the process, I also rejected parts of who I was. I had decided I was going to be different. As a result, I determined to eliminate everything in my life that resembled my family and background. Because my response was born out of pain and bitterness, it eventually led to shutting down parts of my heart and denying who I really was at my core in order to feel worthy. I disconnected myself from my heart and my emotions and convinced myself that I could "do better."

My pursuit to be someone else resulted in me becoming a perfectionist, an exercise addict, and eventually anorexic. I lost touch with myself and began approaching life cold and guarded. I became very bitter and angry, refusing to trust anyone. During this same time, my parents got divorced. Their marriage had been in trouble for many years and this tension spilled over into my life. Although appearing confident and together on the outside, inside I was plagued by fears and traumatized by confusing events.

Upon hearing the news about the divorce from my mom, I felt a sense of hope. Inside my head I was saying "yes I'm finally free," yet almost immediately my heart was crying with deep sadness, longing for love. As I battled about which one to listen to, my head or my heart, I had an overwhelming awareness of my spiritual disconnectedness and lack of inner peace. My ways of coping with pain and life were doing more damage to me than good. I knew something needed to change and it needed to start with me.

As I chose to embrace the process of growth, and pursued a spiritual connection, I came to realize that my perception of life was distorted by my past, my pain and by other people's opinions. As I opened my heart to receive God's love and truth, I experienced an emotional freedom and mental clarity about who I was and what was possible for my future.

Prior to that day, I thought I was doing spiritually okay. I believed there was a God but it was only after this encounter that I realized I had been substituting a religious form for what was intended to be a personal and spiritually intimate connection with God.

I started reading the *Book of John* and became intrigued by the love Jesus demonstrated and the words he spoke when he walked the earth. I remember reading for hours past midnight about this amazing love and how it transformed lives. My heart was filled with a desire to know that love and to love like that. As I continued to read, it felt like God Himself had come into my room, was sitting on my bed, and engaging me in a heart-felt conversation. As I continued to read, it was as if I was looking into a mirror and was seeing the true condition of my heart and my desperate need for intimacy and love. All the shame, anger and pain I had tried to hide within me was suddenly exposed.

That spiritual awakening started me on a journey of learning how to deal with unresolved issues in healthier ways and overcoming blocks to fully engaging life and experiencing deeper connections with others. As I chose to embrace this process of growth and change, I experienced a transformation and freedom that empowered me to live more authentically.

Over time, my heart became freer to receive and give love. Whereas before, I would hide and close off my heart in fear of getting hurt, I was now learning to walk through the feelings of vulnerability and how to trust.

For the first time, I began to feel alive on the inside and started loving myself. The realization that I was loved unconditionally, that I didn't have to be defined by my past, and that I could be free from limiting beliefs, started to sink deeper into my heart and activate waves of healing.

The more healing I went through, the more my relationships changed. My perspective on life shifted dramatically and I began to look at others with compassion and grace. In order for me to be free to live true to myself and experience spiritual fulfillment, I needed to realize that I could never change the past but what I could change was how I was responding to my past. Intentionally choosing to respond differently to painful experiences empowered me to step forward with freedom, strength and unspeakable joy.

Expressing Your Uniqueness

Have you ever seen the Aura Borealis? The first time I saw this phenomenon it took my breath away. It was a cold winter evening when noticed this brightly lit display of color dancing in wavy motions in the northern Alberta's night sky. I had only read about this phenomenon and now I was witnessing its sparkling beauty for myself.

You are like the Aura Borealis. You were created with a combination of talents, strengths, personality and passions that is unique to you. As you learn to live and dance through life more freely from that place of uniqueness, you will display the brilliance of God's glory and others will want what you have. Your purpose will become clearer as you lean into your strengths and live more honestly from your heart.

Living a life of spiritual fulfillment is ultimately about learning how to: Cultivate relationships that engage your heart, become fully connected to God and others, and express your authentic self in such a way that it adds value to the world around you. To become fully alive and free to live this way requires a process of transformation to occur in your heart and mind.

Well-known internet-marketer, Ty Bennett, had an opportunity to meet the late Stephen Covey and was impacted by something Covey shared with him during a private conversation. Covey told him that, "The funny thing about life is that most people think that life is about achievement, - about 'What can I get? How can I grow? What can I be rewarded for?' And the truth is, life is really about *contribution*. It's about helping people. It's about serving people."

Your uniqueness is indeed your contribution to the world around you and by living your uniqueness you express love towards yourself, God and others. The ultimate goal of humans is to learn to "Love God with all your heart, soul and body, and love your neighbor as yourself."

The book of *Romans* says that you have been given gifts that are unique to you and they are given to you for the purpose of serving other people around you. As you become freer to express your uniqueness and operate from that place, you will find that your life inspires and empowers others around you to be fully available to do the same. As they, in turn, operate in their uniqueness, they will empower you. The more you naturally flow in your unique strengths and gifts, the more you will naturally impact others just by showing up and being you.

Cultivating spiritual fulfillment then is not just about you feeling good, it is about identifying who you are, what your unique purpose is and then by living fully you offer that uniqueness to help others around you find strength, vision, and meaning to do the same.

Bio

Lisa Vanderkwaak MSc. is the CEO and Founder of *REAL U Institute*™. She is also a best-selling author, Transformation Catalyst and a Certified Speaking Coach. She is the author of *Let the REAL U Step Forward: 5 Keys to Creating a Richer, More Fulfilling Life*. For more information about Lisa and to receive her FREE Speak to Transform™ Toolkit visit www.LisaVanderkwaak.com

Chapter 20

Why Am I Alive?

By Chloë Rain

December 31, 2011

It is New Year's Eve in Seattle. I had spent my first west coast Christmas, sleeping on the couch of my Aunt and Uncle's home, cutting down and decorating a 10½ foot Christmas tree, while watching, "Its a Wonderful Life" several times. I did not fly back to the east coast to be with my parents for Christmas, (I'm an only child) mainly because I was exhausted by all the plane travel I had been doing on a weekly basis for work. My exhaustion was severe. What I did not know and would find out months later was that I was suffering from an autoimmune disease. My body was attacking itself.

I spent most of the Christmas Holiday sleeping. For New Year's, I had been invited to a party by one of the only persons I knew in Seattle, my hair stylist. I did not know the hosts well and had actually never spent time with Robin and Ray on a social level. In fact, I had never met my acquaintance's partner. I remember Robin saying when he invited me to their house, "you know everyone's going to be gay, right?" I had been single for 4½ years but who's counting? (I am.) I thought, "I don't freaking care, Thank God I won't be alone on New Years Eve."

December, 31st 2011 was actually a beautiful sunny day in Seattle (it is a myth that it rains all the time). I got in my car to get the host a gift for the party. Down the hill from the house, I had discovered this gorgeous little craftsman style renovation that turned out to be a three generation, hand-welded whiskey distillery. I thought a bottle of nice whiskey would be an appropriate gift. Much later Robin and I would laugh at how silly it was of me to think whiskey was a good gift to bring to his house.   He said, "Do I look like a man who drinks whiskey?" Something a bit more refined would have been more apropos.

I took a residential street off the back of the hill in my neighborhood. No one ever mentions the steep terrain in the city of Seattle, San Francisco is known for its precipitous hills, Seattle for the grey skies. No one ever mentions the massive slopes and pitches in the city and the awe inspiring sunsets surrounding the Puget Sound. I came to a stop sign, looked to my right and then to my left and saw a human body smeared across the pavement.

Time warps. I left the seat behind the steering wheel so fast that my car begins to roll and I get back in to throw on my parking brake.

The girl is laying there, head first into the pavement. Her face is obscured by her helmet and her neck and body are crumpled and piled behind the point of impact. It looks like a bicycle accident but I don't remember seeing her bicycle. I will never forget seeing the first drop of blood land on the pavement falling from her mouth. Or the pool of blood that formed under her still obscured face. Blood is black and thick outside of the body. Thick and black even against the dark pavement. She was not breathing at first, because I remember when her breathing began.

There are not words to describe a breath like that, for it's the death breath. It's the unconscious breath that happens when your body has gone into a fight for its survival. It makes you feel as if upon exhaling, those labored lungs may never move again.

Blood and breath. Blood and breath. Blood. I'm paralyzed. Other people are nearby. One of them is calling 911. I stand there looking at her arms. They are thrown about her helmet like pieces of a rag doll that came apart, were broken and became twisted in a distinctly unnatural way. I remember this scene. It feels familiar but not like deja vu. I'm in the time warp were my body is nailed to the pavement. It's as if time got sucked down my mouth and into my body where it's so heavy that I'm rendered immovable.

No one has moved her, because it is obvious that her head, neck, and body are traumatically disassociated. I'm not sure how much time goes by and I don't have anything to do but wait for help to arrive. I get back in my car and drive through the intersection and park on the next block. There, I watch the ambulance arrive. They eclipse my point of view so I can't see her anymore, I don't see them picking her up off the pavement. I wait for them to turn on the lights and screech away at high speeds. Time goes by. I think, maybe they're stabilizing her. More time goes by. Nothing happens. Finally, the ambulance solemnly pulls away. They never turn on the lights or the sirens. I follow the ambulance down the street as it pulls into traffic and goes over the bridge to Fremont. Still no lights. Still no sirens.

I pull off to the side of the road again and lose it. Sobbing hysterically, I call the only person I know in Seattle. He doesn't answer. Then I call my mom in Virginia. I'm losing it, sobbing and crying but I manage to say "Mom, its not me. I'm not hurt." I cry hysterically.

Seven years prior, I had been in a serious motorcycle accident and had totaled my motorcycle when I hit a patch of gravel in a 90 degree off ramp and smashed the guardrail going about 40 mph. I broke both my arms and mangled my full facial helmet, but suffered no injuries to my face. I had 2 surgeries on each arm, donor bone was inserted in to my right arm to help meld the crushed pieces back together. I spent 18 months in rehabilitation and therapy and still have pain and nerve damage in both my arms.

But I never thought much about it. I am fine, my fingers work, my hands work. I walk and I talk. I always joke, "We know how the story ends, I survived. I'm right here." Witnessing this scene, I know. I see. I feel the impact of a life. Its New Years Eve, she had plans. And I don't care if she didn't believe in New Year's resolutions; there's no way that she wasn't thinking about 2012. She was on her way somewhere. Someone is waiting for her. Someone is going to get a phone call. People's lives will change forever. Everything changes in an instant. Life goes like that. One moment you are here, the next moment you are not. The body is a miracle, the heart pumps, the kidney's filter and you never have to think about it.

Until you hit a patch of gravel on the road and you're dead. That's it. New Years Eve 2011 and you're dead. That's it, life is that miraculous and that fragile.

There are only two ways to live your life.
One is as though nothing is a miracle.
The other is as though everything is a miracle.
- **Albert Einstein**

It was like that time Benjamin socked me in the gut in kindergarten when we were waiting in the lunch line because I said I liked him. The wind was knocked out of me and my reflex for taking more air into my lungs had been suspended by the hit. EVERYTHING IS A MIRACLE. There was no other explanation. Before it had just been a convenient saying by an intelligent man, a respected scientist, now it had become an inarguable fact, a law of the universe, a scientific rule. EVERYTHING IS A MIRACLE.

I am alive for a reason. I could have been dead seven years ago. Why am I alive?

I went to the party that night and swore that I wouldn't be the party guest that kept telling the story of the tragic accident she witnessed on her way to pick up a party gift. After the ball dropped, I found myself telling the story to Robin and he, in turn, shared a life-changing story of his own.... we were drunk and talking about life and death. I called the cab company 24 times that night, but in the morning I was sleeping on Robin and Ray's couch in my hot pink party dress.... and as Ray likes to chide me "When I woke up and saw you sleeping there, I knew we were never going to get rid of you."

And that day will forever be the turning point, when everything changed in my adult life. I woke up. I didn't exactly receive a clear download from the heavens above with a to do list and a map.

But I got the message and I want to share it with you. "You're alive for a reason. You better damn well figure out what it is, sooner rather than later. How much more time are you going to waste being half alive?"

I was living a half-life. It was difficult to admit that my career was killing me, and I had few friendships in my life because I worked all the time, and that what I truly desired was to fall in love and be a wife and mother. I had been suffocating quietly under the guise of "having my shit together", embarrassed by my lack of ability to be happy, my lack of guts to ask for all the love I need and want, and my impotence to admit my creative desires.

Finally, a leave you with a few lines from Maude in "Harold & Maude", which is a favorite movie of mine:

"A lot of people enjoy being dead. But they are not dead, really. They're just backing away from life. Reach out. Take a chance. Get hurt even. But play as well as you can. Go team, go! Give me an L. Give me an I. Give me a V. Give me an E. L-I-V-E. LIVE! Otherwise, you got nothing to talk about in the locker room."

Bio

Chloë Rain is your Destiny's Champion, a Personal Transformation Coach, Inspirationalist, Artist Advocate, and Spiritual Photojournalist. Chloë works individually with clients to transform their hopes and dreams in to reality. She also does visual and creative consulting on a variety of platforms including magazine editorials, books, and social media. Chloë had a successful career in hotel development, was a proven leader in the industry managing over $50 million dollars in liquid assets, when as fate would have it, she witnessed a fatal accident on her way to a New Years Eve party. In that moment, everything changed. She started questioning her own life purpose and reason for being alive. She left her corporate career to heed her hearts calling, travel the world, and fall in love.

Chloë now travels the world inspiring others to go for their dreams. Her passion is to help people uncover their blocks and beliefs that prevent them from breaking through, living the life of their dreams, being seen and heard in this world, and experiencing real happiness and success. Her passion and process was birthed through her own journey and process of self discovery, experiencing major break throughs, and yes, ultimately finding herself happy and fulfilled. She is now an active agent of change and evolution in this world. An Inspirationalist and Destiny Champion, encouraging others to find their path, know their truth, and heed their calling. As an incessant student of life, she never stops asking questions and has no fear of delving deep to uncover what's blocking you from your full self expression.

Living on her edge, contributing to the creative force of the world through her work with others, and telling inspirational stories through photography and writing. In her creative work she pairs the aesthetics of natural beauty and the inspiration of life's true stories to convey messages of love and hope. Every picture has a true story behind it - a heart break, a major turning point, an excruciating decision, a moment of grace, a whisper of inspiration, an answered prayer, a new hope, a dream come true, a message for you. It is Chloë's wish to inspire you to trust your inner compass, as she has come to trust her own, to guide your actions in order to realize the fulfillment of your own unique destiny. Every person has a life purpose, and a reason for being alive.

Chapter 21

The Day I Found Out That Fear Was a Fraud

By Kathy Eckhardt

"What would you dream if you had all the resources you needed to accomplish anything you wanted to do and you knew you couldn't fail?"

I'm sure you've heard that question before, but how about this one: *"Why aren't you doing it?"*

Whenever we find ourselves not moving forward toward the life of our dreams, it is usually because fear is grabbing us by the ankles holding us back. No matter what reason or excuse we give ourselves for not doing something we really want to do... at the root of it is FEAR.

"What if they laugh at me, what if I look stupid, what if I fail, what if..., what if ....?"

- Have you ever let the thought that you *might* fail at your endeavor keep you from going for a goal or an outcome that you really wanted?

- Have you ever not done something that you wanted to – something non-monumental like singing karaoke with your friends or getting out on the dance floor to try a new dance style you had never done before or learning how to snow ski, simply because you were afraid you would "look silly" during the learning process and you didn't want to feel embarrassed?

- Has the thought of "what will people say?" ever prevented you from pursuing your heart's desire?

- Have you ever held back from approaching someone at a party or a networking event because that person seemed more confident, more popular or more successful than you and you were intimidated?

- Have you ever been racing headlong toward a goal… all excited and ready to throw your heart over the bar when *somebody* said *something*, either to you or about you that stopped you in your tracks?

Why do we do that to ourselves?

We continue to work at jobs that we hate or that do not pay us nearly the money we are worth but we stay on the job because we fear that if we leave, we will not be able to find anything else. We picture the absolutely worst thing that could possibly happen – happening.

This is called "awfulizing" – Did I just make up that word? No, I actually found it in a dictionary. It means that we create an entire worst-case scenario about a situation in our lives. For example, we think that if we quit the job we hate we might be out of work for a year, broke and living in the street. We imagine ourselves reaching retirement age with no house, no income, no savings and no friends.

Or a woman may stay in an unhappy or even an abusive relationship. Somehow, she has been convinced that she is not loveable and if she left this person, she would be alone for the rest of her life. She makes up an awful scenario. She pictures herself and her kids homeless with nothing to eat and nowhere to go. "At least this is security," she tells herself. So she stays in a situation that is sapping her self-esteem and maybe even, one day, her life. She is STUCK by her own fear.

Would it surprise you to know that it's been estimated that 90% of the things we fear… **NEVER HAPPEN!** 90%! And the other 10% doesn't turn out to be as half as bad as we expected. We did all that worrying for nothing.

Fear is a Fraud!

Let me tell you the story about the day I found that out.

It was at a time when I walked almost every day and my favorite walk took me to a wooded area not far from my house. On that particular day, the sun was bright when I had set out to the woods with a brand new trowel and a big black plastic bag to dig up some periwinkle that I had seen growing there to take back to my garden. I remember that I was wearing a pair of new white slacks... to dig in the dirt... now, WHO DOES THAT?

I entered the wooded area and climbed down an embankment to get to a low-lying, grassy area. At the other side of this meadow, there was a shallow stream with clear, cool, flowing, gurgling water. It was too inviting to resist. I took off my shoes, stepped into the water and started wading up the stream heading deeper into the woods. I had gone farther than I had ever gone before; when I finally decided it was time to head home. I put on my shoes and began traipsing across the grassy area toward the embankment, which was probably about 60 feet to the other side. About half way across, I looked down and realized I could not see my feet. The ground cover I was standing in was not periwinkle anymore. It was tall, almost up to my knees, with big, thick leaves too dense to see through.

Then I had "THE THOUGHT"... if I couldn't see my feet what ELSE was down there that I couldn't see? And suddenly I knew... I KNEW... it had to be a SNAKE! I could just sense it lying right next to my foot. My husband told me I should be careful. My neighbors warned me but I didn't listen. And there I was... STUCK... smack dab in the middle of the field. I couldn't go back and I couldn't go forward. I was rigid with fear. My heart was pounding; my body went hot and then cold. I absolutely could not move. For what seemed like forever, (but was probably only 5 minutes) time stood still. I stood there frozen; knowing there had to be a snake, maybe even a whole family of snakes down by my feet.

No matter that I had been walking in this same wooded area for five years and had never even seen a snake. It was not even snake season. Didn't matter. I was paralyzed.

I could hear the cars rushing by on the nearby road. All kinds of "awfulizing" thoughts ran through my mind like... *"Nobody knows that*

I was going to go into the woods today. I'm going to die in here and nobody is ever going to find me." I felt a fear I had never felt before.

I decided I had to make a run for it but it took every bit of my courage to finally make myself move. I dropped my big black plastic bag full of periwinkle. I dropped my brand new shiny trowel. I climbed up the muddy embankment, sliding down more than once, ruining my crisp white pants. That is how scared I was. But I didn't care, I had to get out of there.

And it wasn't until I was safely back on the sidewalk that I was able to consider what had happened calmly enough to realize that I had created that terror in my own mind. There wasn't any snake. But I had believed the snake was there and so as far as I was concerned — he was there. All of my physical senses told me so. How could I have any doubt?

And now here I was, standing safe and sound on the sidewalk, wondering to myself "What's real and what's not?"

It's like a scary movie. I love movies but I never watch the creepy bloodcurdling ones. And if I do happen to see a movie where the action gets a little too realistic, I cover my face with my hands (though I sometimes end up peeking out through my fingers) until the danger passes. If I am at home watching it on TV, I get up and leave the room until somebody tells me it's safe to come back.

I know, I know… it's "just a movie"… it's not real. My husband tells me that all the time. It's just a made-up Hollywood story and those are actors playing their parts. None of it is REAL. It's simply something someone created using their imagination. Unfortunately, this explanation does not stop my whole body from tensing up. I even squeal at all the right places. The director would be so happy.

Standing on the sidewalk on that sunny day long ago, I understood that in my own life, I'm the director. I am also the one who wrote the script. And of course, I'm the leading lady playing the part. Every minute of every day, I am responsible for all the events in my life. I can create a negative, frightening scenario or I can create a positive, fortunate, happy scenario. And I can change the picture as easily as I can change the channel on my television set. It's all in my mind. It's as real as I allow it to be.

I can write a script full of fear-based emotions like prejudice, self-ishness, jealousy, anger, hate, guilt and shame or I can speak lines of love and joy and promise and hope. I can build my tomorrow by the thoughts I think today.

The world may be being held hostage by fear but I don't have to be and neither do you. We don't have to allow fear to stop us from living our lives to the fullest and becoming all that we were created to be!

"Twenty years from now you will be more disappointed by the things that you didn't do than by the ones you did do." said Mark Twain.

So I ask you again **"What would you dream if you had all the resources you needed to accomplish anything you wanted to do and you knew you couldn't fail?"**

Within your own Heart Center, you have all the resources you need to create the life you have only dreamed about, so as you ask yourself that question, step into the stillness of your heart and listen deeply. Soon the answer will come and you will know what to do. As you begin to move in the direction of your heart's longing, your heart will shout "YES, YES, YES!" and the fear will gradually melt away in response. And one day, you will stand in the sunshine looking around with wonder and realize that you are living the life of your dreams.

Bio

Kathy Eckhardt has been a high-impact performer in the field of sales and leadership training and personal development for 35 years. Her life was exciting, eventful and glamorous. She loved what she was doing and was appreciated and well rewarded. She had it all. Why then did she so often have the feeling that there was something missing — an elusive "something more," that she was meant to do? And why did she continue to attract other successful professionals who felt the same way?

Today, as an empowerment coach, motivational speaker and vision builder, Kathy works primarily helping others, like herself, connect to their deepest calling so that they can do the work they were born to do and create the life of their dreams. As one of the first coaches in the United States trained in the unique Heart Intelligence Method developed by "Britain's Top Coach" Christian Pankhurst, Kathy works with international clients both individually and in small group empowerment sessions.

Kathy is currently writing her first book which expands on the ideas explored in this chapter. Kathy can be contacted through her website www.kathyeckhardtcoaching or www.facebook.com/kathyeckhardtcoaching.

Chapter 22

Attitude of Gratitude, A Spiritual Practice

By Jill Hutchison

"Spirituality isn't something you have one day or not another day.
It's always there. The times when you are feeling less spiritual
are the days when you need to put
more into your spiritual practice, not less."

In my journey, I have powered my way through several courses and devoured many books and programs. I was on an all-consuming quest for knowledge. I sought out thought leaders around the world, travelling far and wide to spend time with them.

Why then, did I start getting annoyed and frustrated? Reading through numerous books on happiness, wealth or success, particularly business success, I noticed the same repetitive message.

When I thought a bit more about it, the piece that was really annoying was what they were saying about gratitude. After all, what did it have to do with business or wealth? How was it going to fulfil me? I was already grateful for everything! (Can you hear my tone - hands on my hips?)

At this point in my spiritual awakening, I realized that if something irritates you, there is normally a reason why. The irritation highlights something you know you should be confronting.

I knew what a good idea it was to write in a Gratitude journal but I wasn't, even though I was telling my clients to do it every day. I just wasn't putting pen to paper. I wasn't finding things to be grateful for on a daily basis.

No wonder it was annoying me! The gap between knowing and

doing was wide open – and it hurt! Nothing annoys me more than when I'm not walking my talk.

I didn't even know how to do it, but somehow I figured it out when I sat down and wrote 30 things I was grateful for. I actually felt the vibration in my body change as I wrote. I started to get excited and realized why everyone had been telling me to do a Gratitude List.

Each line I started with "I'm so happy and grateful...".

Here are some of the things I wrote:

"I'm so happy and grateful for the delicious breakfast I've just had."

"I'm so happy and grateful for the gift of running a retreat in the Game Reserve."

"I am so happy and grateful for the walk this morning, to see the waning full moon as the sun comes up."

"I'm so happy and grateful for the opportunity to work with people all over the world."

What are you grateful for today?

My Gratitude List was just the beginning. I now see it as the doorway to spiritual fulfilment. Being grateful changes the vibration in your body. There is something physical that occurs when you engage every one of your senses in this exercise.

A friend asked, "Does it work to say your Gratitude List rather than writing it?"

Saying what you are grateful for does shift your vibration slightly, but it is easy to get distracted.

By committing to writing at least 10 things before you start, you engage your hand, your eyes and your inner voice while you watch the words form on the page. It is easier to stay focused when you have dedicating time to writing it.

Before, if I would do a list, I would write in such a way that I would close myself off to other messages. Like opening the door, shouting out into the darkness, then quickly closing the door. Now I keep the door open a little longer - to hear what comes back to me. Now my Gratitude List it is how I open my spiritual conversations.

Things began changing in my life… issues I struggled with began to flow and dissolve. Business improved and I was on my way.

When it came to writing my first book, it was obvious in my mind that it would be my Attitude of Gratitude Journal. So at the end of 2012 – there it was.

It wasn't until I was having a blissful escape from the rigours of life with our teenage family on a secluded beach in Western Australia that the world really changed. My book mentor sent me an email asking me why I wanted to write another book. I decided to grab my notebook and sit on the warm autumn sun, toes buried in the sand and write about why I wanted the next book.

I asked the question.

There it was again – that other voice.

It was an amazing experience! The kids were hungry, I got a bit sunburnt but I kept on writing. The words fell out of me so fast I could hardly keep up with them.

That first day was uplifting, enlightening and miraculous. I would ask a question and an answer would immediately come to mind in a voice that was not mine.

Sometimes I would question whether this was my imagination or was I making it up. I was in the perfect place where I did not have to be anywhere or do anything so I just kept with it.

Who or what is that other voice? I call "it" God because I had a religious upbringing. I also realize that other people may be put off by that name, depending on their own beliefs and backgrounds. It makes no difference what you call "it"; whether you think of it as the Universe, Energy, a Higher Power, Universal intelligence or your inner voice, gut feeling or intuition.

At first it was exciting. Then it got a bit freaky! Pretty amusing when, for over 40 years, I've been praying to God, asking for answers, believing that he answered prayers – but then when He spoke back at me it almost scared the daylights out of me!

After one day of writing, He asked me if I wanted a message and immediately I was overwhelmed with fear. This one question pushed me right up against my terror barrier. What if the message changed the way I perceive the world around me in a way I would not like? What if He asked me to do something I did not want to do?

I realized that for over 30 years I have kept busy so this voice would not bubble up and ask me these questions. Every now and then, I would hear it and take note of it. It was always so clear and so close to the truth that it often felt surreal.

The closer we get to truth, the more we tend to shy away from it. It's like a light that's really bright.

We make ourselves busy, it's sometimes easier than listening to the message we most need to hear. It gives us an excuse to keep on going without thinking too deeply.

I'm busy. Isn't every parent who has a business and three children?

I write every day. I ask questions that are burning inside or ones that just pop into my head. I comment on what I observe around me. Sometimes the answers are inspirational, sometimes cryptic and sometimes they are a bit scary.

Some answers kept popping up, so I thought I would share the list I have compiled so far:

1. Keep things simple.
2. Decide what you want, and do not second-guess it.
3. Pursue what you want.
4. Pursue what you know is nudging at you, what you know is right, even if it seems illogical.
5. Smile, breathe, do yoga, talk to your plants.
6. Sit in the sun every day. Fill your solar cells.
7. Expect an answer. Wait for it and listen to it.
8. Trust your intuition.
9. Focus on what you want, do what you can – then let go.

We are forever seeking fulfillment. Materialistic things fill the gap for a while. Relationships with others fill the gap for a while. It is when we acknowledge that we are spiritual beings having a human experience that we find *true fulfillment*.

It is by doing what we know, rather than talking about what we know, that things come together.

Using a Gratitude List to get us into the right frame of mind assists us to tap in and truly listen to the messages we need to hear.

I'll share with you one of my recent conversations:

God: What do you do to find fulfillment for yourself? Not just for others, as I know you love to organize things so others are fulfilled – which doesn't always fulfill you.

Me: But hang on, I thought spiritually mature people found fulfillment in selflessly doing things for others? Oh gosh, I thought I'd run this one out of the park. I know perfectly well this isn't true. True fulfillment comes when we do activities that fulfill us AND our values, which may include others finding fulfillment too.

God: But it starts with you. Which, paradoxically, is not selfish, but the best gift you can give to those around you. Do you know what fun you are to be around when you're feeling fulfilled? Do you know the energy you radiate? It's enough for others to live off for a week.

Me: So you mean the world's got this back to front? They say, "You'll get fulfillment from being of service to others." When it's really supposed to be "First find fulfillment yourself so you can be of service to yourself and others". That's pretty profound!

I trust that you are inspired to start writing in your own Attitude of Gratitude Journal, every single day. And that it opens up a whole new world of conversations that you may have known were there, but just out of reach.

Relax into being a student of life, knowing we will never have all the answers but that we are allowed to ask lots of questions.

Bio

Jill Kean Hutchison is the author of the Attitude of Gratitude Journal, a business owner, investor, wife and mother of three wonderful kids! She is known as the mentor that takes successful, driven individuals into their next power, the one they have been struggling to see and tap, the one that will throw open the doors to their next opportunity. Connecting individuals to their most powerful selves, and assisting them in shifting attitudes, beliefs and actions is what gives her energy. Seeing their eyes light up when they 'get it' is all part of the journey. For some it's been about creating their personal guidelines and money rules, for everyone it's been about getting clarity on what they really, really want. Having grown up in South Africa and moved to Australia with her young family, she has experienced many challenges that she took in her stride. Staying true to her values and constantly questioning what life was all about, Jill inspires all who listen to her and assists them to find opportunities wherever they are.

Jill currently lives in Perth, Western Australia, with her husband and children. With a background in the Financial markets and certificates in Life Coaching, Master Results Programming, Corporate speaking, Ericksonian Hypnosis and a Batchelors Degree in Economics, Jill has a solid foundation upon which to draw.

To order your Attitude of Gratitude Journal please visit www.jill-hutchison.com/spiritual. Jill's blog and regular Chooseday message can be found on www.evolvedynamic.net. Put your details into the box on the right hand side and you will receive free regular inspiration and thought-provoking messages. Connect with Jill on Facebook: Jill Kean Hutchison

Chapter 23

Discovering Spirituality By Embracing Humanity

By Genevieve Prono

There was a time when I thought I did not fit in. I believed I had come on earth either too late or too early. I would have loved to be a pioneer discovering unknown lands or an astronaut shooting through the stars and the galaxies - in search of other planets that had generated life. But I was stuck in the present where I felt awkward and out of place. In retrospect, my journey looks like a treasure hunt. At some key moments, I would be handed pieces of a puzzle that would lead me further on. It was not until entering the new century that I have come to realize that I am exactly where I have always been meant to be: walking people through transitions at the beginning of a new spiritual age.

The first piece of the puzzle I was handed was how I entered the world. It became a legend in my family. I was born in a little clinic in Aix en Provence (France). My father was fighting in the Algerian war while my mother lived back with her family. I arrived weeks early, weighing less than two pounds and had to be resuscitated at birth. The odds of becoming a healthy child and adult seemed grim. My grand-mother took the lead of the operation. She put me in a shoebox, filled with cotton to keep me warm then rushed me to Marseille's hospital where the very first incubators had made their appearance. I did the thirty kilometers ride in a taxi after my uncle's car broke down. I stayed there three months - the tiniest and the most determined baby in the ward. Nobody except my grandfather believed I could make it, but I did. Soon, I was strong enough to finally be in the arms of my mother.

Fast-forward a few years for the next piece of the puzzle. I had grown to be a tall and skinny five year old. I was curious, eager to learn and so happy to be in school. My enthusiasm inspired my teacher to put a little four year old boy who had difficulty adapting to school under my care. I probably did a good job because he was soon like a fish in the pond.

A year later, I was faced with another piece of the puzzle. While I was healthy and full of energy, I did not resemble the chubby children that were the norm at the time. Our family doctor suggested to my mother that a stay in a center for children in the Alps would help me to develop more of an appetite. It seemed a good idea at the time: my mother was about to have an operation for her back, my grandfather was ill and the rest of the family was mobilized around him. I could be taken care of while benefiting from the pure air of the mountains.

What was not foreseen was that during the six months I stayed there, I would be treated badly and humiliated. I would be left in front of my plate almost at every meal until I had finished eating it or it was time for school. I was faced with the choice: spending the entire recess alone in the refectory or forcing myself to eat and being scolded and punished for throwing up.

Another difficulty I had that made me a target was that I started wetting my bed every night and even dirtying my pants. I remember having to carry my dirty laundry or clothes around the dormitories in order to "show my shame". Phone calls were not allowed and our mail was filtered so I never got a chance to tell my parents what I was experiencing.

I was not the only one treated badly. I quickly found myself taking care of children in need and in pain. They would be drawn to me I guess because they felt my strength (which I didn't feel).

I, of course survived and once the six months was over I returned back home. My family had moved to the States in Arlington, Virginia. This was the beginning of a new era. In three months I had became bilingual and because I was from a different country, there was a noble reason why I was different. Eventually, this difference faded because I blended myself into the scenery. Even though I had the same white-blond hair and blue eyes as some American girls and I had developed a Virginian accent, I still did not fit in.

The next piece of the puzzle was the birth of my brother. I had been waiting for him for so long. My mother had been so traumatized by the circumstances of my birth that she did not want to try again. It took the experience of a friend who had jumped the step of a second baby after a traumatic birth (and my ongoing requests!) to convince her. I was twelve years old and I was going to be a big sister. I was in joy. This was ecstatic: if that dream of a baby brother could come true then everything could come true. I just needed to ask long enough.

The next pieces of the puzzle were the births of my children. I have always wanted a large family. I remember being 5 years old and saying I was going to be like the famous French writer of children's book, La Comtesse de Ségur, who had eleven children.

I was 24 when I gave birth to my first son by an emergency cesarean after 28 hours of labor though I had wished for a natural birth. I felt stunned when I was told "one cesarean, always a cesarean." Then, more bad news to my large family dreams as my doctor told me that after two pregnancies I would have to have my tubes tied. Even though I was blessed with that little boy and so happy to have him in good health, I was devastated. My whole belief system had been shattered. I could no longer have the belief, which I had inherited from the legend of my birth, that I was a survivor. I would contemplate the fact that if I had lived in those historical periods I cherished I would have probably died as well as my baby. This, to me, was unbearable.

I entered a period of depression. I could not help consider that my body had failed me again, like when I was in that center in the Alps. I could not come close to windows or had to push my back to the wall in the metro because I feared the impulse to throw myself in the void; not because I wanted to end my life but because of some sort of hypnotic fascination. That scared me so much. Miraculously, breast-feeding helped me create the bond that had not naturally emerged because I was separated from my baby at birth.

I wrote a lot to put some order to all my tumultuous thoughts and feelings. I had started a diary at age 10 and it had been such a comfort through each difficulty. I discovered shiatsu and made some changes in my eating habits and gradually I came out of the depression. I then made the decision to ignore the doctor's allegations of "one cesarean, always a cesarean" and try for a natural birth with my next child.

Two years later, my husband's work brought us in Iraq. Pregnant with my second child, I found a woman doctor that seemed confident with my situation. The pregnancy went very well but the outside conditions were difficult. The country was at war. The hospitals had shortages of personnel and supplies. Near the due date, I was alone in Bagdad with my son while my husband was working up in the north.

I was having on and off contractions and made the error of going into the hospital too early. I was sent back home twice and the third time I was gently persuaded by my very kind and understanding doctor to accept a second cesarean again under general anesthesia. I had the promise there would be no tubes tied. I woke up with my baby in my arms, my first girl.

Back in France, three years later. I had to see twenty different doctors before I found one that was ok with trying a natural birth after two cesareans. Unfortunately, he was on vacation at the end of my pregnancy. The doctor he referred me to was reluctant. After an intense two-hour discussion, I surrendered and accepted a third cesarean. I only had my desire and my gut feeling, no data, nothing to back my logic and my demands. My beloved mother had died during the pregnancy, my best friend and my husband did not understand my quest. I was alone and could not face the idea that something could go wrong because of my perseverance. I had negotiated quite a few things and the cesarean went very well.

I was awake for the first time, under epidural and my second little girl never left me. I was assured I could have a fourth baby if I wanted. It was only a few days after that a huge wave of anger swept through me. I made the oath that I would never be tricked into doing something against my inner knowledge again.

I had decided to discover how things work when they go well and why they had not gone as intended in my case. Because I set the intention to keep on doing the research until I found the information, the Universe handed me many other pieces of the puzzle. I came across people, organizations, books, articles and finally had access to the knowledge I had lacked. One thread naturally lead to another.

I went back to school, studied natural birth, psychology, alternative medicines. I discovered meditation, did a lot of introspection and continued writing.

It gave me the strength to find the people that would believe in me and let me try again. I finally gave birth naturally to my second son three years later, my third daughter six years later and my fourth daughter eight years later.

Fighting this battle all those years gave me more than my dream for a large family of six children. It evolved me. It taught me how to get out of my head and connect with my body. I learned to trust, nurture and cherish it. I developed my intuition. My experience helped me cleanse belief after belief, uncover and heal the wounds of my past. It gave me a larger purpose in life. All along my quest, women would come to me because I was a little ahead of them on a similar path. They asked for understanding, comfort, help, information, guidance and support. I felt propelled to go even further so I could meet their needs.

The puzzle is not finished and I hope there will be many more pieces I find along the way. But those that have been assembled show a clear picture. Not only do I fit in but also I am exactly where I should be in this time and space. Making friends with my body and accepting my humanity has helped me discover the spiritual being inside of me.

Bio

Psychotherapist, coach, holistic healer, speaker, facilitator, trainer, author, Genevieve Prono has been helping women and men for 25 years at key moments of their life and during periods of transition and change like pregnancy, entering parenthood, separations, traumatic experiences or changes of orientation. She was a La Leche League leader from 1988 to 2005 where she had positions at the International level, founded and was the first president of Cesarine (www.cesarine.org) another nonprofit organization, co-founded Doulas de France (www.doulas.info) and started her own company in 2002: Chrysalide France (www.chrysalidefrance.com). She also trains and coaches health professionals, social workers and alternative professionals and has been doing that for fifteen years. She is currently writing a book both in French and in English "From one birth to the other – overcoming cesarean and preparing for a VBAC" (Vaginal Birth After Cesarean).

Chapter 24

Leaving a Spiritual Legacy

By Paige Arnof-Fenn

In that past few years I have lost my mom, stepdad, and both my in-laws. I have sat with several close friends as they courageously battled various forms of cancer. There is something clarifying about facing mortality and with each of my friends and family, I found it very interesting that the topic of legacies came up time and again.

The discussions ranged from "What's it all about anyway? I thought by this age I would've figured it out already" to "Why am I working so hard with no end in sight?" to "Does anybody other than me really care if this succeeds?" to the stated desire that the world would be left better because of a person's presence. Personally, I find the concept of leaving a legacy fascinating, especially since I don't have any offspring, which most people believe is the natural way to leave a lasting mark on the world.

How do you know if your life has been successful? You've probably heard the saying, "You get what you measure"—so how do you decide which metrics are the really important ones to watch? In business you can look at the ROI, sales revenue, EBITDA, stock price, cash flow, etc. Each of these benchmarks is important for different reasons, and depending on what question you are trying to answer, any of them could be a relevant response.

When I started my company more than eleven years ago, my main concerns were about filling the pipeline with interesting client work. Would there be enough work to keep my colleagues busy and interested? Could we maintain the quality and culture that we were known for as we scaled and grew? Would it still be a business I want to run?

I started this business with the goal of working with people I respect and admire and for people I want to help succeed. I wanted more autonomy, flexibility and control. The funny thing is, I'm working longer and harder than ever before, but it feels different when it's your firm that you're building. I'm starting to think more about what I want this company to be known for in the market. I didn't start this business with a specific revenue target in mind, but I know growth is critical both personally and professionally.

I've realized that the metrics that matter to me most are not the typical entrepreneurial concerns... I think while we are still here, we can create a *Spiritual Legacy*.

Downtime for Extra-Curricular Activities

I wanted to start a business I could leave when I went on vacation and not worry about or let consume me so that I could relax and enjoy myself. (When I'm on, I work all the time, but when I take off, I really want to wind down.) I wanted to have time for community involvement and advisory board work, which I never seemed to be able to squeeze in as an employee.

Work-life balance is not a concept I understand well. I knew my business was real when I took a vacation the first year after starting it and new business still closed while I was away. They were projects I'd been trying to convert, but the checks didn't actually arrive until I was out of town. In fact, every time I've taken a vacation, a new client has signed up. I take that as a positive sign that the organization can survive and thrive without my intervention at every step.

Recharging your batteries is critical, and I know I'm more effective and creative as an entrepreneur when I get out in the real world, away from my office and my computer. Making time for family and friends keeps me in touch with reality and helps me make better decisions. I've been able to find time to coach a group of inner city entrepreneurs, and it's been incredibly fulfilling to share my experience and lessons with them. It's inspiring to watch them grow their businesses and learn from the group.

Staying True to Core Beliefs

Loyalty is one of my core values—loyalty to self and to others whom I respect. It's important to me to gauge how many colleagues and customers come back and refer us to those who trust them. Being true to the mission of the organization and delivering superior experiences matter to me a lot. Having the confidence to walk away from a client or colleague who's diluting the equity in your brand is tough but it's necessary sometimes. You must always be authentic to the essence of your brand and surround yourself with people who reinforce your brand and its values—not tarnish it.

Here is what really matters to me: Relationships matter. Quality encounters matter. Honesty matters. Consistency matters. Authenticity and integrity matter. The experience and the journey matter. Focus on what matters to you and get rid of things that don't. Taking the clutter out of your mind and your life frees up space for more of what you value.

Success is very personal so your definition will be (and should be) different from mine. To me, growth for growth's sake is meaningless, but profitable growth with interesting clients solving important problems is what keeps me engaged and excited. The ability to spend time with people I love and care about is critical. My reputation really matters, and the positive word-of-mouth means a lot to me since almost all of our business comes by referral.

So how can you measure these things like quality and experience? I used to conduct customer satisfaction surveys when I worked for large companies, so I know research is important but are there more tangible ways to see if your clients are benefiting from your work? I've been asked by a client to join his company's board of directors. Another client introduces me at meetings as his business consigliore ("She may tell you she's a marketing consultant, but I don't make an important business decision without talking to her first!").

A great quote about success comes from Ralph Waldo Emerson:

"To laugh often and much; to win the respect of intelligent people and affection of children; to earn the appreciation of honest critics and endure the betrayal of false friends; to appreciate beauty, to find the best in others, to leave the world a little bit better, whether by a healthy child, a garden patch or a redeemed social condition; to know even one life has breathed easier because you have lived. This is to have succeeded."

I once read a proverb that said if you lead a meaningful life, you never really die. Instead, you break into 1,000 pieces, each of which stays alive within the people whose lives you have touched along the way. I like that concept and often think about who those 1,000 people would be in my life. My family and close friends would certainly make up a large piece of it but I hope it would also include my mentors and mentees, team colleagues, fellow board members and even strangers who were touched by my articles or speeches or had shared a cross-country plane ride conversation.

I'd much rather be remembered by a few dear people on rainy days or as the friend you could talk with for hours in front of the fireplace, in a coffee shop, on the phone or on warm days when taking a walk rather than having my name on a building. Making a lasting impression on the people who mean the most to me is what I really care about and I want to be remembered for: being kind, warm, sincere, generous, unique, special, funny and fun.

I do not know who said "Do not fear death so much, but rather the inadequate life," but I think that sentiment is true. I want to be remembered as a multiplier, someone who raised the level of play of everyone around them, who always created positive energy in the room and sparked new ideas.

A good rule of thumb to help guide you in life when you are trying to decide which path to pursue is to take a longer view of your options. So do you attend the wedding of a close friend or agree to speak at a prominent industry conference the same day in a different part of the country? In 10, 20 or 50 years, who will remember or care about the decision you make? Going through that exercise can help clarify priorities quickly.

You can leave a legacy or lead one - it is your choice whether you are passive or proactive here. Thinking about this topic in my 40s, I now realize the choices I make every day with my time and my calendar directly impact how I'll be remembered. Who I spend my time with and how we pass that time together really matters. I will never get those moments back again, so I want to make sure I spend them wisely.

I hope it will be many decades before we find out what legacy I leave. I still have a lot to accomplish. I think my biggest opportunities to make a difference and have an impact are still ahead of me. I want to change the world in some important way and know, before I leave, that it is better because I was here.

My company is the platform from which I operate daily so now that I am thinking about these things, it occurs to me I do not have any succession plans in place. Like many entrepreneurs, I have been so busy building my business that I did not make the time to think about the bigger issues like who will keep my dreams alive without me here. I think the secret is to include others in your big dreams so even after you are gone, they continue to expand and reinvent themselves in relevant ways. That way, your spirit will live on.

The old saying that it is amazing how much you can accomplish if you do not care who gets the credit may apply to leaving a legacy as well. Your good work and good deeds live forever in the hearts and minds of those you touch along the way. Remember those people who've left lasting impressions on your life and share the lessons they taught you with others this year. What a wonderful and memorable gift for this year and beyond.

Bio

Paige Arnof-Fenn is the founder and CEO of Mavens & Moguls, a global marketing strategy consulting firm whose clients range from early stage start-up to Fortune 500 companies including Colgate, Virgin and The New York Times Company. She was formerly VP Marketing at Zipcar and VP Marketing at Inc.com before the company was sold to Bertelsmann. Prior to that she held the title of SVP Marketing and was a key member of the IPO team at Launch Media, an Internet start-up that went public in early 1999 and was later sold to Yahoo.

Arnof-Fenn has also worked as a special assistant to the chief marketing officer of global marketing at The Coca-Cola Company and held the position of director of the 1996 Olympic Commemorative Coin Program at the Department of Treasury, U.S. Mint. Previously Arnof-Fenn worked in brand management at Procter & Gamble.

Arnof-Fenn is a founding Board member of Women Entrepreneurs in Science & Technology and she is the past Board Chair of the Alumni Board of Stanford University. She is the representative for Harvard Business School on the Harvard Alumni Association Board, which governs all the schools across the university. She is also the former Vice President of the Harvard Business School Global Alumni Board and the current Chair of the Board of Trustees of the Sports Museum at the Boston Garden, is an advisor to several early stage private companies and non profit organizations and is also a 3 time past president of the Stanford Club of New England which serves alumni in a 5 state region. She holds an undergraduate degree in economics from Stanford University and an MBA from Harvard Business School. She is quoted regularly in the media, was a monthly columnist for Entrepreneur and Forbes for several years, is on the IDC Technology Advisory Council, and a Time Magazine Opinion Leader.

Chapter 25

Overcoming Adversity:
The Spirit Knows No Limits

By Janette Moore

I love waking up and not having to rush into an office. I enjoy my mornings, meditating, my coffee, yoga, taking my best friend to the dog park and then starting my workday. I know that I am truly blessed for I can work from home.

It was not always that way. I remember what a grind it was to sit in traffic just to be in an office for eight hours and then sit in more traffic to make my way home. Traffic was not my only struggle. I had internalized much of my childhood. I used to believe that I could not succeed at anything because my mother told me many times at a young age that I was not wanted and that I was an accident. She told me that God did not want me and that nobody wanted me. I felt that anything that I did I had to do it on my own, partly because I was a perfectionist and partly because I was afraid of failure.

After college, I married, had a beautiful daughter and twelve years later went through a divorce. Now it was up to me to raise and support my daughter. I did not realize that this was going to be a gift from the universe to challenge me to discover my passion and purpose.

It took me some time to realize that it was the fear of feeling pain that kept me stuck. I sabotaged my own success by making no movement at all. I was an expert at denying my experiences. I had inherited issues that caused me a lot of emotional pain. I learned that sometimes what shows up in life is not always what you wanted. Sometimes less than ideal things happen. Sometimes your idea of who you should be gets in the way of who you are. I realized that most of my life, I had been living in a fog.

In one year, my life took a drastic change. I started taking Neuro-Linguistic programming (NLP) courses. NLP gave me intense focus and a crisp sense of clarity where I could forget myself, lose track of time and help me to feel part of something much bigger than myself.

I discovered meditation, which brought yoga into my life. All three of these ingredients helped me understand myself better and most importantly helped me forgive my parents for my childhood. Forgiveness opened the space for me to discover my career choice. I realized if we want to make a difference in the universe, we have to become the best version of our self.

I realized if I could make other peoples lives better, then I have a business. I wanted to create a product providing a service. I started up my own Inspirational Coaching practice helping others and with that my life shifted and doors started opening. Not to say it did not come with some new struggles. If I had known what it would take to start my company, I probably never would have done it. When I did, I became obsessed. When you are obsessed, you keep trying until you make it happen.

I found what really lights me up is giving others value. The more I give out, the more value comes in. Remembering this has helped me to get through the challenges of running my own business and enjoying life more.

Overcoming Adversity

My Mantra in Meditation:
Ask the Universe,
My Angels,
God
Use me to do what I am suppose to do

Let Spirit Tell You When

My business taught me many spiritual lessons. I learned we cannot wait until we have "everything." By that I mean we cannot wait until we have mastered the best website, the best flyers, the best manual. We have to jump right in. That is where things will come to us. We will learn from trial and error. You may find that what you thought will work may not be of any value to your business. We have to step full in and start giving what we have. This is when we start receiving and you will notice your clientele will shift. The key is to be aware what is working, what is not working and make minor adjustments as you move along. DON"T STOP! Do not listen to the negative voices when someone does not agree with your product. Make the adjustment and keep moving. Be completely organic!

Invest In Yourself

We, as women and men need to figure out our own self-worth. When we invest in ourselves is when doors open. Hire a Coach, a Mentor to keep raising your knowledge and positivity. Besides, if we are not committed in investing in ourselves, how can we expect our clients to invest their money with us?

Money Beliefs

Sweet Mother of Cookie Dough… I am so grateful that I transformed my relationship with money. I took six months to work on my money issues around charging for my services. Once I changed my mindset, I found my worthiness. Now, I am valued and deserve to be paid for my great services.

Anyone that believes that money is evil or that anyone that is rich is either bad or just lucky, needs to work on this negative belief. Money can provide freedom and security. It offers countless opportunities to make a difference in the world. Having financial stability beats being broke any day. Most of all, being able to monetarily help others… this the freedom I want to share with others.

In the beginning, I would take four steps forward and then six steps back. It was a negative paradigm. Do not be afraid of charging for your services or raising your prices. I came across this in the beginning of my start up. I had that "inner voice" telling me that I was not good enough or had some "tire kickers," tell me "who do I think I am for raising my prices?" It is the snarky voice in your head that likes to mouth off whenever you think about being bold or more self-nurturing.

Money is not a limitation. Money is just an idea. If you want a lot of money, come up with many ideas. Pursue those ideas but make sure that you can see yourself staying with the plan until its conclusion. If you cannot see it, do not pursue it. Successful ideas cannot be successful if you can't see it to the end. You need to believe in your product and believe in yourself.

Money Affirmations are important. Some affirmations that I use:

- I am valued
- I'm worthy of myself
- It's ok for me to have an abundance of money
- I am a success
- I let go of fear
- I give and receive money easily
- My financial success is a testament to universal love
- I attract money
- I'm well compensated for my work
- I live an abundant life with money, health & happiness
- I can be spiritual and show others how to be successful
- I feel peace when I manage my finances
- I respect money
- I'm a good steward of wealth

Daily Spiritual Journal

Keeping a journal to write about your accomplishments. Writing about what I am grateful for on a daily basis has been so rewarding for me. When you look back and read where you were a year before and where you are now it makes you realize that all the hard work does really pay off.

Building Spiritual Community

Something that I have learned over the years is realizing that my list of clients is like "Money in the Bank" and building that community is important. Engage in your list and be consistent by showing up as the authentic successful person that we stand for. Remember there will be growing pains but know that it too will pass as you learn and constantly grow. We need to keep ourselves on course. Daily routine is crucial to staying on course. Our beliefs are our reality. I came from enduring chronic depression to being fulfilled in my life. I have a beautiful daughter that looks up to me and am very proud that she admires me. Playing small does not serve the world. We are meant to shine. Everything we have right now, we have created.

Bio

Janette Moore is an Inspirational Coach whose life ambition is to encourage people that there is no such thing as "I can't or I shouldn't." She is a graduate of SRI University, Certified NLP Strategist and Certified Market Psychologist. She lives between New York & Toronto with her hilarious dog, Oakley, who has become the first dog to escape from any leash, fence, and actually believes that he is the NEW Houdini. Currently, she is writing her first book "Between Me And You", a free-lance writer developing blogs about Inspirational Love, Healthy Recipes, and how her life turned into an "Inspirational Life".

Chapter 26

Lessons Learned Through My Mother's Love

By Margaret Cowles

My life's journey revolves around my mother who passed away seven years ago. She had been bravely battling Alzheimer's for 10 years. I was her primary caregiver. Caring for someone who had always cared for me was something that had never crossed my mind. A part of me was ripped apart as I watched the daily losses Mom suffered as she slowly slipped away.

Alzheimer's was cruelly stealing pieces of her mind each day. I realized that I had to seize every bit of life, hope, and love before she was gone.

I have always loved stories. I recall listening with wide-eyed wonder as my Mom told me about her life. She spoke of growing up, her early years and her life. I especially loved the stories Mother told of my Father. Some stories are easy to hear, some hard. Others, I had to live with for a while... allowing them time to sink into my body and mind. Then there are those that leave me still wondering. But none are without meaning. These stories have provided me with strong roots as well as wide and clear perspectives.

We took countless walks through the woods. She always said nature is a place of peace, refuge, and natural beauty... a gift for our soul. She always said that nature speaks to our hearts and help to restore our internal balance. Mom shared how answers to many of life's questions can be found simply by communing with nature.

Everywhere we look life is constantly giving us hints regarding how our time would be best spent and how to make the correct decisions. Signs help to make our lives better but listening for and heeding them are choices we must make each moment.

I think we always know what is the best authentic choice but sometimes we just don't follow through. Signs constantly lead us wherever we go. We just need to make a point of paying attention and listening to them more often. We need to open up to our inner voice. We all have the special ability to hear the direction our intuition gives us regarding what we are meant to do in life.

Mom pushed through and conquered many hardships and struggles during her life. She did so bravely and gracefully with the help of God and the love and support of a great husband. She always put other people before herself. I truly believe that demeanor is what helped her overcome every challenge that life threw at her.

As I lived through the final 10 years of Mom's life while she suffered with Alzheimer's, the stories were a reminder of what was real and what truly mattered. These memories brought me to the understanding of where I was supposed to be.

I believe that our experience is about expressing spirit in flesh to the greatest degree possible and to learn to love and accept ourselves unconditionally. We are all unlimited spirits facing life's limitations.

How strange that it took this mind-robbing disease to bring so many memories to mind. As I looked after my Mom, I recalled her caring for me as I grew up. We took garden lunches and long walks in nature. My mom loved her flowers and herbs. Her gardens were always thriving and expanding because of the care she gave them, much like the care she gave us growing up. They say plant a seed and a miracle will happen. The miracle lives on in Mother Nature. I so relate to this as how to run my business. My mom has and always will be my greatest mentor!

My journey through her life stories is an inspired one. Her greatest teachings may have been in those last few years when she could no longer hold sentences together. There were times when she seemed unaware that I was with her but that didn't matter. I sat by her side and brushed her hair just as she had done for me in my youth. It was then that I became the storyteller. I repeated the stories she had shared with me throughout the years. As she lay there, staring at me, I just knew somehow she was taking it all in. I felt her contentment in listening to the recollections I was repeating. She seemed to know that they would be passed on and her teachings would help touch another heart or two along the way.

I explained what was happening in my life. I told her how beautiful she is. I expressed to her how gifted and loved she is. I thanked her for being in my life; for being my mom. Mostly, we held each other's gaze with love.

I was with my Mom when she passed away. She lifted her sweet head, and looked to the other side of the bed, where no one stood. She then looked at me and hugged me. She did that twice. It was miraculous! For the previous two months, she had been paralyzed in her body and couldn't move on her own. Her body and mind had grown listless and tired. Yet, even as she was drawing her last breaths she was giving one final lesson. Even when facing impossible odds a spirit filled with love and determination will prevail. With one more glance towards the other side of the bed, she lay back down and closed her eyes. She was gone. She had left this world just as peacefully as she had lived in it.

I know my Dad was waiting for her on the other side of the bed. We talked about that a lot during our times together. She told me Dad would say that if he went first he would be waiting on the other side so they could carry on where they had left off.

I appreciate and respect life; however I also respect death. It can be beautiful or it can be very difficult to witness. It changes you as a person.

I know that I live a lot by intuition. I tend to take unusual actions that don't make sense to those around me but they often see that my life has a strange way of working out.

In a way, I'm building stories. I believe that when we integrate the body, mind and soul, we access the intuitive part of ourselves that knows where balance and peace resides.

I'm a problem solver by nature. I lead my life with my heart and let it lead me from within. Life works out best for me when I don't ask "what if?" but ask instead "what can I do with it?" When I allow intuition to become my intention and take action while remaining detached from the outcome, great results tend to come. I may not know what they're going to be but when they arrive, I absolutely recognize them as being what my heart wanted.

I trust my journey and declare that I am open to all events occurring along the way to help me in ways that I may not understand at the time. As I remain open to receiving, I also remain deeply grateful for the process every step along the way.

I'm so very grateful for your stories Mom. You have taught me to live with spirit as my guide. Here's to you Mom! Thank you for knowing who you were. I am grateful for your trusting spirit and teachings along the way.

Through my life I have read countless books and attended endless seminars and lectures. All of them put together couldn't make a dent in the strength, wisdom and knowledge which my Mom passed down to me. I can only try to be half the woman that she was. I miss her each and every day. During some of my hardest times in life, I have smelled her perfume and actually felt her touch as if she was stroking my hair. I know it is not my imagination. I believe it was my Mother offering what she knew best, how to give love and compassion. My world is a much better place because my Mother was in it.

Bio

Margaret is very driven to be successful in life. She is the CEO of Lifestyling By Design. And partnered with Maureen G. Mulvaney as Co-Founder of The Women's Millionaire Club. She decided to create a life of fullfillment. She is just a down to earth small town Michigan girl who dreams real big; she went for her goals; got a little lucky and alot of her dreams have came true. She feels blessed and not a day goes by that she is not thankful for my friends, failures, and successes. The most important thing is that she loves is to laugh and make others laugh as well.

By her late 30s, she had become a Savvy bussinesswoman, website designer, lifestyle coach and inspiration to men and woman around the globe. Working part-time from home, while caring for my mom with Alzheimer's and Parkinson's. She is a multi-dimensional success. She transforms entrepreneurs and empowers men & women; and is an inspirational to budding business owners taking their beginning steps on a path toward grasping prosperity. Her deep understanding of the keys to success combined with her heartfelt compassion is a genuine true reaction in everyone who listens. She maintains a demanding schedule of personal activities as well as a series of web sites, each offers insights, newsletters and products designed to help individuals achieve their personal best. Remember... Let your journey begin.

Chapter 27

Breaking Through Life's Lessons

By Melody Shin

As long as I can remember, I've been in love with babies. When I was a teen, I volunteered as a junior leader at the local YMCA summer camps to care for preschoolers. I always knew I'd love to be a mom one day. I always imagined that I'd have girls and how fun it would be raising them, especially because I loved spending time with my mom and sister. I love doing girly things with them and I didn't particularly enjoy masculine boy stuff.

So when I first found out I was pregnant, I was ecstatic to finally be a mom! I didn't care of the gender, and I was truly excited to give birth to a healthy baby boy.

Then I got pregnant again and gave birth to another boy. Hmm... well that's ok I thought, I really loved being a mom to two little boys.

Then the third baby came and I thought this HAS to be a girl, right? I mean, what's the probability?

I guess third time is *not* the charm for I had another boy. I was bitter and angry and disappointed at the ultrasound. How could this be? What's wrong with my husband's sperm?

I started a quest (or to some, a rampage) to find the answer. It made no sense to me. I really wanted a girl. Every cell in my body was screaming for a girl.

There must be a reason why I only had boys and I was going to find out why.

My research did not reveal quick answers. It wasn't a type of food or the Chinese calendar or a specific position.

I searched and was unable to discover anything that made sense to me.

Finally, one day, I heard a whisper from deep within me.

"You're a leader," it said. What? Me a leader? Nooooooo! How can I? I didn't know it but a small fire had been lit on my quest for the truth.

The desire to serve had always been strong in me. I had always been driven to create and to share. I had founded a Waldorf homeschool group and taught many moms and children. But, I had a belief then that it was too hard to manage it all. Surely, I should be happy just being a mom. I will send my kids to a good school like the rest of the world and go about my every day life.

I decided I needed a spiritual outlet so I started a blog and expressed my deepest truths.

Now don't get me wrong, I was completely in love with my baby and I of course realized there's really no difference whether I had a boy or a girl. But, I continued to seek for answers and to try making sense of this world.

Then I hit a low point in my life. I decided to pull my kids out of a highly esteemed private school. Pulling them out meant leaving all the comfort and familiarity we had known. It meant leaving all of my friends and the life I had created. But I had to take a stand for my children and listen to their needs. I had a deep desire to honor my gut, that keen mother's intuition, that something was not right and I must stand for my children's need for freedom and healing. (I now realize that the law of attraction had co-created this in order for me to step into my true self!)

This was truly my biggest lesson in my life and a turning point. I had to muster up all the courage I had in order to be a voice for my children. Do I go along with the crowd and hope that things will improve and settle for what is? Or, do I recognize the strong pulls and choose to take a leap into the unknown territory?

Well, I chose what I knew it to be true. I chose to rethink education, to rethink life, to rethink myself.

I left my life, as I knew it. And even though I knew I did the right thing, I felt such deep sorrow and went into a deep dark hole.

Then after a while, I had a choice to make. Do I stay feeling sorry for myself and fall deeper into depression or see it as an opportunity to try something radical?

But to be honest, I really didn't know anyone remotely inspirational in my life. All I could do was to wish that I knew someone successful and inspirational. The internet is a wonderful thing. And, YouTube is phenomenal. I'd watch videos and felt the loving warmth of a mentor cheering me on.

Then it happened. I found an answer to my seeking. I found a mentor and a tribe of women from around the world, successful gutsy women following their dreams and changing the world. I immediately jumped in with both feet!

I had stepped into a space that was different from anything I knew before. And almost instantaneously, my family was given a new opportunity to start anew. My husband got a job offer to move us to New Jersey, 7 minutes from Manhattan. We were open and ready! Everything seemed to happen all at once.

All of my boys had been born in Los Angeles, so this was a huge move for us Californians but I was starting to see a glimpse of deliberate co-creation in action and was super excited for this new life.

We found an amazing house, a dream house that was almost three times the size of our Los Angeles house. We met amazing friends right away and formed a wonderful tribe around us. My family loved the lush green nature of New Jersey and truly felt the high of an adventurous life together.

Then, I got pregnant again.

I thought, of course it's a girl this time, right?

I mean, come on!

Nope! Hello to my beautiful curly-haired pumpkin baby boy.

Ok, this time I got it. I got the message. Finally! I really did.

If I had a baby girl, I would not be writing this story. I'd be shopping for some cute frilly pink thing. I kid you not! I wouldn't be masterminding with other brilliant game changers from around the globe, I'd be busy decorating a cute little pink room.

You see, I had made a contract. I've come to understand that I had chosen this life as my higher self before being born. I now believe that we all do.

I had made a contract that I would complete my purpose and

mission on this world and I'd get a big nudge to bring me back if I got side tracked.

And having four boys is one of those nudges.

It's different for everybody, though. Have you felt a nudge in your lifetime? What purpose were you reminded of?

I couldn't have imagined that having four boys would ignite my fire to find the true goddess within me. Who knew? If you had told me this when I had my first baby, I would not have believed you. When I had my first son, I was at a completely different place in my life.

Another low point in my life happened when I was about 6 months pregnant with my first baby. I had a great career as a graphic designer for a motion picture advertising firm in Hollywood. It was lunchtime and since it was payday, I stopped by the ATM to get some cash. Instead of having over a thousand dollars deposited automatically into my account, my cash request was declined and my account showed a negative balance!

What? How is that even possible? I was devastated and humiliated because my co-worker who came to the ATM with me had to lend me money to buy my lunch. What I didn't realize was that my husband and I had a huge debt and the credit card company had taken my pay as soon as it got deposited.

Never again, that is what I thought; never again will I feel like I can't feed my unborn child! That's when I realized that I needed to find a different way. A different way of thinking and doing things that was different from what I was taught… by school, by parents, by society.

You could say that it was a huge wake up call. Do you listen to yours? I know that I didn't always listen to them. However, I ALWAYS notice them. The trick is paying attention when they occur. Now, I watch and listen to them very carefully.

Each baby helped me to discover an inner power I never knew I had. Having four boys gave me the inner courage to honor my heart's desires and to finally live my life on my own terms. It was not until I had four boys that I **knew** there was a clear purpose to my life.

Bio

Melody Park Shin is an international mompreneur. She is passionate about empowering moms to create the life they truly desire, in parenting + marriage, health + career. She gives away her Manifesting MOJO Formula on her website so that more women can begin to live their heart's desires.

Melody follows her heart's desires and currently resides in South Korea and Hawaii with her four boys and husband. Living life on her terms, Melody unschools her four boys by honoring their passions and traveling the world in style.

Melody truly walks her talk, and is a master at implementation. She can help actualize your dreams and make it a reality!

Chapter 28

Finding Fulfillment in a Higher Power

By Carla Burke

"The best day of your life is the one on which you decide your
life is your own. No apologies or excuses. No one to lean on, rely on,
or blame. The gift is yours – it is an amazing journey – and you alone
are responsible for the quality of it. This is the day your
life really begins."

~ Bob Moawad

From time to time, the powerful forces of earthquakes, tsunamis, hurricanes and terrorist attacks shake our world. These events often cause the deaths of hundreds, sometimes even thousands of people. Afterwards, many attempt to explain these tragic events as God's punishment while others ask the classic question: Why?

In Psalm 46:1-5 the psalmist wrote, "O God... I will take refuge in the shadow of your wings until the disaster has passed." The psalmist also indicates their struggle in the face of tragedy, describing life in terms of darkness and despair but also holding out hope for God's salvation and deliverance.

Just this week, as I was writing this article, I heard the news of the bombings in Boston. It is hard to avoid the doubts, fear, and questions that come into our minds. We naturally think about our mortality and all the "what if's" that can happen in our lives when we step out the front doors of our homes. The answer to many of these questions cannot be to lock ourselves in our homes and never leave. So, what is the answer, and how do we get through these tough times?

I often reference 1 Peter 4:7-11 where he says, "love each other deeply, offer hospitality to one another, use whatever gift you have received, faithfully administer God's grace, and serve... with the strength God provides." The author is telling us to keep being the light that God has created us to be in this dark world every day. We cannot stop the evil that is in this world, but we can be a source of hope and light, by continuing to be faithful in love and serve God with our whole heart.

The Lord does not promise us a life without strife. On the contrary, we will all go through hard, rough times at one point or another. God says in James 1:2 to consider it joy when we encounter trials. Notice that God does not say if but when. The Christian life is a life full of trials and tribulations. God takes us on different paths to bring us closer to him and more like Jesus. However, when the trials do come we can remember that we are only passing through the bumpy time for a short while and that God is with us. Knowing that Christ is with us transforms our struggles and us. Our faith steadies us.

One thing I know for sure is that people, places or things cannot fulfill me. No amount of friends, no amount of traveling and no amount of clothes, shoes, purses or whatever else we hold dear on this earth will ever fill me up like God does. This did not happen to me overnight. In fact, it has taken many years of God pruning me into the person I am today to realize that God is the most important thing in my life. Without Him, I would have nothing.

It is like pruning a tree. You have to cut away all the old stuff so growth can occur. In my case, I needed to get rid of a lot of things which has allowed me more time with God, more time to read and more time to spend with my loved ones.

I recently began a huge endeavor of cleaning out and giving away items I no longer need. I had accumulated so much that I had become over-saturated and none of it made me happy. In fact, the clutter made me unhappy.

I grew up in a Military family and so I was used to moving every couple of years, which made it easy to throw out the old. For many years, I continued the habit of moving often after graduating college.

Now, after living in the same house for eleven years and raising two children, I was feeling overwhelmed by all the clutter. Every time I turned around there was another room to de-clutter! Each room took an exorbitant amount of time. That is when I realized… we do not need a lot of things to make us happy. In fact, my home was making me unhappy because I had cluttered it up by filling up my life with objects. God is the only one who can fill my needs and my heart.

The chaos that clutter created in my life tripped me up not only physically, but also mentally and spiritually. Clutter can really affect spiritual well being. (If you have ever tried to have your quiet time surrounded by clutter, you know this is true.) Hebrews 12:11 teaches: "No discipline seems pleasant at the time, but painful. Later on, however, it produces a harvest of righteousness and peace." Make sure the spot you have designated to spend time with God (or whomever you call your Higher Power) is free of debris that may distract you.

The more time I spend with my Higher Power, the more it makes me want to be a light. Being a source of light means being there to help others in need and not turning a blind eye. Taking a meal to a sick person, visiting someone in a nursing home, volunteering time at your child's school or at a charity of your choice, or serving in the church such as volunteering to help with Vacation Bible School are all examples of the many ways we can be a light. It does not even have to be church related. These kind acts might not seem like much but God sees every act of kindness we do. God is not looking for people who make headlines; God is looking for those with faithful hearts. Being a light means, what am I doing for Jesus and how can I be more like Christ? I think being Christ-like makes us more compassionate, peaceful, humble human beings.

Even if you do not believe in a Higher Power there are several things you can do to pay it forward and spread joy.

1. Buy groceries for someone in need.
2. Offer up a parking space or let someone get in front of you in heavy traffic.
3. Volunteer your time.
4. Give a bottle of water to a workman that leaves your house.
5. Smile and say thank you to servers.

Give because it makes *you* feel good. Giving is contagious! An old Chinese Proverb says that one joy scatters a thousand griefs. I know how true this is after I started volunteering my time helping special needs children ride horses. Years of grief and sadness over one thing after another were lifted from me as I stopped focusing on my problems. Talk about being fulfilled! There was nothing better!

Remember you cannot reach for anything new if you are full of yesterday's junk. Give, give, and give some more and you will live a more fulfilled life.

Bio

Carla Burke is an award-winning Author who won The 2011 Christian Literary Award for her beautifully written and illustrated children's book, "I Spy a Dragonfly". She lives in San Antonio, Texas with her husband and two children. Her children and her love of nature with a particular fondness for dragonflies inspired her first children's book. Her second book combines her love of horses and children and tells a very important story of how children are affected by life-threatening food allergies - mainly peanuts and tree nuts. The story is told through the eyes of a pony named Peanuts and his owner named Penny who has to be careful with everything she eats because she is anaphylactic to peanuts. That means that if Penny eats even a trace amount of a peanut or tree nut, then she only has about 8 minutes to live. She carries her Epi-Pen with her wherever she goes to ensure that if she accidentally ingests peanuts or tree nuts, a shot of an Epi-Pen into her thigh will save her life. Carla appeared on The Review with Joy & Company, a local TV show in Dallas to discuss her books.

Carla graduated with a BA in Journalism from the University of Texas at Arlington and has written numerous short stories and articles for local newspapers. She is currently working on her third children's book about how therapy horses help children and adults with special needs. The idea came to her when she started volunteering at The Saddle Light Center for Therapeutic Horsemanship over a year ago. She has put in many hours taking care of horses, shoveling the stalls, grooming the horses and helping the children she works with ride horses. The children love Carla and look forward to seeing her and the horses week after week for the lesson. She has seen the children thrive during their looks forward to helping them. Carla is also on the Fundraising Committee for this non-profit organization.

Carla is also working on book about surviving and healing from suicide. In memoriam of Carla's brother, Jay Clark McMurdo who hung himself at the age 44 on May 17, 2005 and Mason James McCoy (who was her best friend's son) who shot himself in the head at the tender age of 14 on March 11, 2012.

Chapter 29

The Grace of Unconditional Love

By Davina Ilgin, PharmD

I was so excited! My grandparents were visiting from India and we were on our way to show them the Sears Tower (now the Willis Tower) in downtown Chicago. At the time, I was just 8 years old and it was the tallest building in America. As we were exiting the car, I was just staring up in awe at the amazingly tall building when all of sudden, "Bang!" went the car door and "AHHH! Ouch!" I screamed. My finger got stuck in the door jam! My older sister did not realize I was coming out of the same car door as her and slammed it right on my finger!

My grandmother immediately dropped to her knees and started to pray. I couldn't believe it! She was praying instead of opening the door! I don't think she realized that my finger was stuck... it all happened so fast. Dad came running around the car to open the door and save my poor finger. Luckily, it was still intact.

I remember laughing about it later - not about my finger being crushed but how my grandmother fell to her knees in prayer instead of opening the door. Growing up in a household with little spirituality or religion, I was dumfounded by this type of behavior.

Although my grandmother was a very religious woman, none of her three sons carried on her legacy of strong faith. My grandmother had an 8th grade level education and was a homemaker. Her husband, my grandfather, was a very intelligent, highly educated and successful engineer who happened to be an atheist. My dad and his brothers emulated their father becoming successful engineers who all ran away from faith and religion.

I was taught at a young age that everything is possible if you work hard. I worked hard in school and graduated with honors in high school and college. I worked hard at playing the organ and won the state championship. I trained hard at volleyball and made the team, despite being the shortest girl trying out. I believed that I had total control of my life and all of my goals were attainable.

Although I achieved many accolades, the number one goal in my life was to become a mother. I had it all planned out - I would get married at 25, have my first child at 27 and so on. Well, I met the man of my dreams in college and married him soon after graduating... precisely at 25 years of age. Piece of cake, I thought... now, we will have kids!

Becoming a mother turned out to be the most challenging time in my life. Month after month, the pregnancy tests came back negative. Every month that I got my period felt like a failure. Then, finally, over a year of trying to conceive, we finally saw those two little lines and just like that, we were pregnant! I was elated! My dream of being a mother was finally coming to pass.

Unfortunately, life had other ideas as soon after, I miscarried.

I was devastated. It was the first time in my life where I was not "in control". I remember crying hysterically on the operating table after the doctor removed the remnants (and my hopes and dreams) from my uterus. "It's not fair! We worked so hard for that baby!" I cried. I just did not understand why this happened I blamed myself.

After grieving for some time, we started trying again. Months went by and every test came back negative. I was out of my wits by this point. I felt helpless. "What if I never become a mom?" I thought.

After another whole year of trying, we finally got a positive test. Eureka! I'm going to be a mom! I found out soon after that we were having TWINS! My grandmother had twins but I never thought in a million years I would too. They say it skips a generation.

We were ecstatic! Twin boys. I felt redeemed. I lost one child and now I am going to have two at once. In my mind, it was sort of like making up for lost time. I did not even think of how difficult it might be to carry and care for twin babies.

As mothers, we dream about and idealize our birthing experiences. I pictured my twins swaddled in soft flannel gently placed on my breast to hold, ever so gingerly because they would be so tiny and fragile. We would bond instantly. I would nuzzle them lovingly while inhaling the soothing and tender fragrance that only babies emanate.

Once again all my plans were cast aside when my water broke early. The harsh reality of preterm labor and an emergency C-section *three months early* robbed me of this most precious dream.

Instead, my twin boys were rushed to the Neonatal Intensive Care Unit (NICU). I was not able to see them nor hear their cries because they could not breathe on their own. They were more than tiny - Milan weighed a wee 1 pound 12 ounces and Shaan was just 2 pounds 4 ounces.

As with the miscarriage, I felt cheated again. How could life deal me this unfair hand? My babies were torn from me, lying prone in their incubators in an intensive care unit!

After our traumatic delivery, the nurse wheeled me into the NICU. I was drugged and an emotional mess. Tears welled up when I saw my boys struggling to stay alive - with tubes and wires hooked up all over them. The medical staff were poking and prodding our tiny, helpless little babies while the breathing machines were pumping air into their lungs and long orange tubes were placed down their throats to deliver milk. Even with all of this, a sense of pure joy wafted over me from the depths of my soul when I saw the indelible faces of my precious babies.

Moments later, I was lost to sheer panic and fear. I moaned and mourned—would they be handicapped? Will they make it? Why had it come to this? I wanted to see their first steps, hear their first words, celebrate their birthdays, teach them how to read, watch them ride their bikes; raise them to be kind men.

"Will they survive?" I asked my husband. Being the rock that he is, he answered with a faithful, unwavering "Yes!" I wondered how he could be so strong and so sure.

Then one of boys fell very ill. He had a serious infection. The docs told me they needed to perform a spinal tap to rule out an infection in his brain.

I watched in horror as they punctured his tiny back with a large, long needle. He had no anesthesia! He could feel everything! Although he was tiny, his cries were ear piercing. It was not right. I am his mother

- I should be protecting him and I could not. I felt helpless once again.

I wanted to pour my love into him. As I watched him endure this unimaginable pain, my heart broke and I realized in that instant that he is our little miracle. He was so precious and dear to me. I would have given my life for him. It was the first time I experienced the truly unconditional love of a mother for her child.

It was so much to bear. In an emotional rage, I ran to the pumping room nearby and wept. Something, some one brought me to my knees. With tears flooding down my face, I prayed a desperate plea to God to show mercy on my son, "Please, God, help Milan! Take away the pain and infection! Be there for both our boys in this time of darkness. Make them healthy and whole. Make them healthy and whole. Make them healthy and whole. Please, God! Amen."

When I finished that prayer, I realized that my son's crying had ceased. My fears suddenly evaporated and a sense of peace flowed through me. I was not alone. My son was not alone. It was not up to me anymore. God was in complete control and was taking care of my baby. I had not felt this peace for a long time. In that moment, I understood the unconditional love of God.

From then on, prayer became part of my daily life during the emotional rollercoaster ride that lasted 14 long weeks. We were hit with an onslaught of bad news - our son might have cerebral palsy, our other son will need surgery, they were plagued with pneumonia, and so on. I was able to relinquish control and walk in faith for the first time... and it led us out of the darkness. Our boys, now 4 years old are healthy and whole, cured of all ailments.

It wasn't until years later when I pondered over the trials we faced as a family that I can really understand how God or the Universe works. I realize now that *every* experience in life, especially the challenging ones, are there for us to grow spiritually. Our faith is put to the test in the area of most importance to us. In my life story, it was motherhood.

God lightly tapped me on the shoulder with the negative pregnancy tests month after month. I did not heed the lesson. Then he nudged me with the miscarriage. I still did not *get* the lesson. I did not grow from those obstacles. He finally forcibly pushed me to my knees with my boys' premature births.

He did this for me to get to know Him, His grace, and His unconditional love. He gave me the strength to endure and grow. I finally *got* it; and I am eternally grateful for the experience. My grandmother's sons may have not inherited her faith but, like twins, it skipped a generation.

Bio

Davina is an Author, Mentor, & Pharmacist. But she is first and foremost, a Mother. She lives and breathes her motto, "Let's change the World… one Mommy at a time." Her three amazing boys were the impetus to founding Mommy Life Coach Academy, where Mothers learn to be the best Mommies they can be and have a positive impact on their children, and ultimately the World.

Contact Davina at mommylifecoach@gmail.com and visit her at www.mommylifecoach.com

Chapter 30

Seize Your Purpose and Take Ownership of It

By Dr. Beverly A. Crockett, Ph.D.

There are those that search a lifetime to find what has been defined as fulfillment. This is probably one of the most sought after, life changing events ever known to man or woman. By achieving it, one may believe they have reached the pinnacle of success. Some search for it in wealth or riches. Many try to find it by acquiring businesses, companies, properties or other tangible items. I'm compelled to propose to you that one important aspect of fulfillment comes from discovering who you are spiritually. The word 'spiritually' by definition means: Of, relating to, consisting of, or having the nature of spirit; not tangible or material; as distinguished from the physical nature. We can now begin to understand that we have at least two distinct parts to our being; natural and spiritual.

Let's first address how you came to be who you are and where you are. It is significant to note that you are not a biological accident. You were placed in this world with destiny and purpose. Discovering what that is and how to obtain it is most rewarding! Acknowledgment of the One that created you, in everything you do, brings you into the alignment with the Creator. There are promises that were made on your behalf before the foundation of the world and once you tap into them, half the journey to fulfillment is complete! There is a Proverb that says, "Trust in the Lord with all thine heart; and lean not unto thine own understanding. In all thy ways acknowledge him, and he shall direct thy paths." In other words, there are things that are going to challenge the very foundation of who you are; things that you will not understand. We do however, have an opportunity to trust our Creator for direction and counsel to assist us in making decisions, even when we do not understand what we do or why.

The roadmap to finding fulfillment in this spiritual age first starts with having a positive mindset. It does not mean that negative thoughts don't come to mind. It does mean that the manner in which you choose to channel them is key to fulfilling your purpose. You must stay focused on what you are designed to do. Purpose is what brings satisfaction to the very core of your being. This allows you to move from ordinary to positive thinking and overcome the struggle with the negative factors in life.

Everything that you propose to do in this Spiritual Age begins with your mind. Our thought processes often determine the final outcome of situations we encounter on a daily basis. The mind is our greatest battlefield. Whatever you **think** you are in your heart (your mind and heart are connected) is exactly what you are!

In the current state of the world, you cannot afford to have an ordinary mindset. Ordinary has been defined as: of no special quality or interest; commonplace; unexceptional, plain or undistinguished; somewhat inferior or below average; mediocre, customary; usual or normal. The mere fact that you are seeking fulfillment is an indicator that you are far beyond ordinary; in reality you are extraordinary!

There is however an emotion that may be crippling you and causing you to be stagnant or immobile; thereby leaving you in a non-forward thinking mode. Fear is an emotion that tends to leave one feeling powerless, vulnerable and defenseless. It is something that hinders progress and impedes growth and success. I believe replacement theory is necessary to overcome fear. Learning to utilize other emotions such as joy, satisfaction, happiness, expectancy and courage help us to face our fears and develop positive images of doing the very thing that can catapult us into purpose.

Inner strength, ambition and confidence are all attributes that are necessary for daily, victorious living. I am a firm believer in whatever state your mind is when an event, tragedy or situation occurs has much to do with how you perceive it and proceed.

My humble beginnings did not particularly line up with the structure of the All American Family partly because I did not have the benefit of having both parents in the home. Nevertheless, I had a hard working, loving mother and doting grand and great grandparents. As I matured, I was grateful for the blessings I had received on championing myself through life's woes and struggles. I had been groomed to adjust my attitude to accept the circumstances of each day. Learning to trust that someone was always going to be there for me came through the wisdom the adults in my life were so willing to share. Through them I was taught to know that no matter what happens in this life, I will overcome my challenges for I can do all things through Christ which strengthens me! This helped me to develop the philosophy that, "I AM A CHAMPION!"

Paul the Apostle shared his personal experiences with us... he declared that when you do good there is an evil force that is always going to be present. Believers and non-believers alike are challenged in this area. He talked about his desire to serve God wholeheartedly, but everyday life caused him to not always be the person that he desired to be; the man that God said he was. This is the war in the spirit as he describes it. "But I see another law in my members, warring against the law of my mind, and bringing me into captivity to the law of sin which is in my members." You see, in Pauls' mind, he had the fear and the admonition of the Lord; he had godly principals that he was "trying" to live by, but there was a constant battle going on and it was in his mind! Paul started out as a persecutor of believers and ended as a noted author. Through much adversity, Paul was able to triumph over those battles and went on to pen some of the most powerful writings ever read! This is proof positive that where you have been is not as important as where you are going!

You too, can become victorious in everyday life. When you realize that you are created in the image of God in His likeness and because you have dominion over everything in the earth realm, you cannot fail! Push past the obstacles and hindrances that you see. Have faith in God and know that "Faith is the substance of things hoped for and the evidence of things not seen!" I believe in "Spiritual" things that I have been taught through the word of God. It solidifies the fact that I am a champion; particularly when the vicissitudes of life tend to weigh me down.

In all honesty, a champion is not an ordinary person for that would merely be a "winner." A champion perseveres through tests and trials that are faced daily through the deviations of life. Depending on your age you may have heard of a cereal that used as a slogan, "the breakfast of champions." I believe that we have a spiritual breakfast of champions that includes weapons of warfare. We have to develop what I'd like to term "tools of a champion." These tools come in the form of reading and studying the scriptures, prayer, worship, fasting and praise unto God!

What has stood out more than any of the phrases used within the definition of the word champion was one termed, "war games." In life, as we run this God-ordained race, we encounter many facets of war. We have enemies that are seen and some that are not. We must <u>always</u> develop and activate a strategy that will enable us and in the end, cause us to triumph over and through the snares and traps that have been set.

I would like to submit to you that you too can overcome any challenge or obstacle. I would like to bring to light a human example in today's time and that would be Mrs. Michelle Obama, wife of the President of the United States of America. Mrs. Obama is a living example of a person who has found her purpose. Though she started out as the daughter of seemingly middle class parents, she is now living her destiny as a wife, mother daughter and national spokesperson for many great causes. She is yet facing all criticisms, but still fulfilling the role she was called to.

How do you find fulfillment in the spiritual age? Might I suggest that once you find your purpose and discover your destiny, fulfillment is just around the corner! Don't miss your moment!

SEIZE Your Purpose! - TAKE Ownership of It!

BE Your Purpose – LIVE On Purpose!

Bio

Dr. Beverly A. Crockett is a native of Columbus, Ohio and received her formal education there. She is a Magna Cum Laude graduate of International Seminary, based in Plymouth, Florida, as well as a graduate of Gospel Lighthouse School of Ministry, based in Columbus, Ohio. She also graduated Summa Cum Laude from Ministerial Training Institute in Inglewood, California were she received a Bachelor's Degree in Theology and a Master's Degree in Biblical Counseling in July, 2005. Dr. Crockett received a Doctor of Philosophy Degree in Biblical Counseling under the direction of Dr. Johnny J. Young, Ph.D. from the Ministerial Training Institute, in July 2007. She graduated with Summa Cum Laude honors. Additionally, she has completed coursework through Greater Life Evangelistic Ministries and Columbus State Community College in Computer Technology.

She has been the Executive Director of the Moreno Valley Community Education Center, an extension of the ministry. A portion of her assignment has been to recruit, interview and train qualified volunteers to mentor and tutor in the after school intervention program along with the ESL and the GED preparation class at MVCEC. Pastor Crockett has previously served the President of the Ministerial Alliance, Church Administrator, Praise and Worship Leader, Sunday School Teacher and a member of the Board of Directors.

Her passion is to teach and train people of God to empower them with leadership skills that will be a tremendous asset to the Kingdom of God. Another area of ministry in which Pastor Crockett is passionate is counseling, specifically grief and family and pre-marital counseling. Dr. Crockett is naturally gifted in the area of writing and editing and released her own book in August, 2008, "Just Run The Race." Her second book, "Just Run The Race – You Are A Champion!" is due to be released in 2013. She is also a much sought after conference speaker and workshop presenter with a primary focus on leadership, about which she is passionate. Professionally, she is the CEO and Founder of Executive Business Writing of which editing, preparation and proofreading of potential manuscripts is a main source of assignments.

Dr. Crockett is the mother of one daughter and grandmother of three grandchildren ranging in age from 6 to 20 years of age. Her philosophy is regardless of what befalls one in life, Champion Status is obtainable.

Chapter 31

God's Gifts

By Cynthia Turner

Sometimes you don't know God is all you need until God is all you have. I know what it's like to have to completely trust God. In my lifetime, I have experienced rape, domestic violence, divorce, toxic mold illness, the death of my mom-all of which I thought would take me out each time. Yet, each of these experiences contributed to the woman I am today. I thank God for bringing me through these traumas.

Through all these traumas in life, I have become an encourager to others in similar situations. Daily I try to maintain a positive attitude. I'm not saying everyday there is nothing to get under my skin but I am saying I make a choice to find something positive about that day to say. I thank God for my mother and father that instilled God and positive thinking in me as a child. It's good to go because your parents tell you but it is great to go when you have that personal relationship with Him.

As I walked through difficult times, I uncovered my voice. I now love to share how God helped me and how He can help you. I remember when I used to get into trouble in school for talking all the time. Now I know God gifted me that way from the beginning. Through my pain, God converted my love for talking, music, and helping others into what I call a ministry/business. It allows me to pursue my career that offers the flexibility to spend time with my family.

God leads and guides us to become what He wants us to be, in spite of our past. When we find out the purpose for being on this earth, it is our duty to go out and do it. You must do as Matthew 6:33 says, "Seek ye first the kingdom of God, and his righteousness and all these things shall be added unto you." No matter what we do in life, place

God at the head of it. We can't ask God to bless our plans; we must ask God to plan our blessings.

Hardships bring so many things to light that we otherwise may not have been aware of. Hardship reveals things within our heart, such as impatience, doubt, and frustration. Regardless of the circumstances that each of us face, the Lord's purposes are singular. It is to draw us into Himself and to reveal His deep love and unending provision.

Times of struggle get our attention for they press deeply into our heart, mind and spirit. The Lord's desire is to get our attention and both our eyes directly on Him. When this happens, we are looking to God to be our provision, our all in each and every circumstance. Also, when our eyes are set in His direction, we will see what He gives us and our hearts will be encouraged to believe and ask for more and more from Him alone.

Even though circumstances, people and things will come and go in our lives, God is the one immovable anchor that will never forsake or abandon us. There isn't anything that we can do that will cause God to leave us. His love never fails us and He desires us to rise up to His challenge to trust Him. He wants us to surrender, lay down before Him, believing that He will make a way and in the midst that He will comfort and carry us through.

There are things I can suggest for people going through trials right now. The first thing I would suggest is get a relationship with God (not just a Sunday walk-in/walk out experience either) It should include a prayer life where you take time out of your day to pray for you, your family, friends, associates and your enemies. Yes, I did say your enemies. I have to admit it is not easy at first, but if you want to grow, you need to do those things. Next I would study the word more. Open up the bible more than when you take it to church on Sunday. If you can go to bible study, that is where you can learn to apply the word to your everyday life. Also I would say go to conferences and events where you can grow.

Take it upon yourself to learn and grow. You can't have the attitude of I know it all, because you don't. You can't grow in God, if you are unteachable. While you are at that church make sure you serve in some way according to your spiritual gift. It is always good to give back to help others using your time, talents and resources to humbly serve in the church.

Surround yourself around positive things. Make sure you have some real friends. Value quality over quantity when it comes to friends. Ask God to lead people to you that are for you. Ask God for guidance in all that you do. He will surely send people to help you and direct you along life's journey. Take time for other positive things, some would call these things the little things. If you're a single mother like me, sometimes that's just sitting at home by yourself is a true gift. It can also be just a simple walk, going listening to some jazz or poetry to relax. These things are important to balance you.

Practice forgiveness. That right there is a big one for me. I've been hurt by people and situations. For a while, I carried that hurt around everywhere I went. You can hold on to that unforgiveness where you hate everybody and everything that hurt you. It wasn't until I forgave that God allowed me to heal. Everyday it gets easier and it is a process to get over pain. I thank God I've learned to deal with people that hurt me in a better way now. Remember you may never get that apology from the person that hurt you. You have to go on in your life because usually that person has gone on with their life, and you are still stuck in the hurt from the past.

Our obedience is a key for the access to all God has for us! There may be times that you truly wish He would write it on a white board what he wants us to do. God gets the glory, and it opened doors for different opportunities for my business. I've learned that when you turn it all over to the Lord, He truly works it out!

Bio

Cynthia Turner is the CEO of MsCynt LLC. She is a marketing/PR/business consultant for businesses, nonprofits and ministries. She is a "networking queen" who never meets a stranger. She attended Alabama A&M University and graduated from Faulkner University with a Bachelors of Business Administration. She loves to teach businesses how to market and brand themselves online and offline through the power of social media and connections.

Cynthia is a rape, domestic violence, and toxic mold survivor. She has a passion of encouraging others and telling the goodness of God. She has a radio show, called The MsCynt Show, where she loves to interview inspiring people from Christian entrepreneurs, authors, musicians, singers, groups, motivation speakers. Cynthia lives in Birmingham, Alabama as a WAHM (work-at-home mom) of two daughters. There she gives back to the community in several volunteer positions dealing with the homeless, economic empowerment, poverty alleviation. She has a local website called Birminghambizguide.com where local companies can advertise their businesses and display their discounts, sales, and events.

She loves people and loves God. Some of the things she loves are: love to laugh, music, fast cars, theatre, plays, sunshine, water scenery, horseback riding, hiking, racquetball, playing cards, and spending time with her family. Find out more about Cynthia and her business, MsCynt LLC and connect with us on social media. Visit her website at http://www.MsCynt.com MsCynt.com. Like us on Facebook at facebook.com/MsCyntShow and follow us on twitter at twitter.com/MsCynt

Chapter 32

How Jesus Taught Me Self-Esteem

By Patricia Samuels

I have healthy self-esteem. I get this healthy self-esteem from Jesus. I know that may sound odd to some, but when I think about his goodness towards me, I cannot help but love him and myself. I will explain more in a minute, but first let's look at this verse of scripture:

Surely he hath borne our griefs, and carried our sorrows: yet we did esteem him stricken, smitten of God, and afflicted.
But he was wounded for our transgressions, he was bruised for our iniquities: the chastisement of our peace was upon him; and with his stripes we are healed.
- Isaiah 53:4-5

Before we get into this verse, let me just mention why there is such low self-esteem among women. A vast majority of women do not hold positive images of themselves. They do not know who they are, nor what they are worth. They continuously make unhealthy comparisons of themselves with other women and then magnify the areas in which they feel they do not measure up. In large part, society is the culprit for this behavior. Society bombards us with images of what is supposedly the goal we are all to achieve. Every woman on earth is supposed to look like Barbie™ and anyone who falls short of this is doomed to failure. If the truth be told, many of the "Barbies" of this world are insecure, believing that in many ways, they too do not measure up. They see themselves with flaws, which in their eyes, are larger than life. There is no reason for any woman to fall into this "I am less than" category.

The scripture given above is our ticket out of low self-esteem.

In this passage, we find Isaiah prophesying about the crucifixion of Jesus. In addition to alluding to the crucifixion of Jesus, Isaiah also implies that we did not have sense enough to even realize what Jesus was doing by dying on the cross. Instead of understanding the work of the cross, it says we believed that God was punishing Jesus. We believed he was stricken, smitten of God, and afflicted by Him. We, or more particularly the people of Jesus' day, believed that God was punishing Jesus because they thought Jesus was impersonating the Messiah. They did not believe that Jesus was the Son of God, because he did not come in the manner that they had hoped. They thought he would come in an obvious, powerful, and kingly manner and would immediately wipe out all of their enemies. While Jesus did not come in the form they had imagined; Jesus was indeed powerful and destroyed the works of the enemy. While there are many who recognize that Jesus is the Messiah, many still fail to recognize and appreciate the true meaning of the Crucifixion. Many of us live beneath our privilege, because we do not know what Jesus died for us to have.

> My people are destroyed for lack of knowledge.
> - Hosea 4:6a

In order for us to have a healthy self-esteem, i.e., know who we are and what we are worth, it is imperative that we understand the work of the cross. God allowed Jesus to die on the cross on our behalf as an exchange for us to have eternal life and *an abundant life* on earth. He allowed Jesus to be wounded for areas where we have fallen short of the mark, and bruised for any premeditated sins. Please notice the colon (":") in the verse. When a colon is inserted in a sentence, it is to signify that the words following it will explain the words preceding it. Following the colon in this passage, it states that the chastisement of our peace was upon Jesus and with his stripes, we are healed. Jesus took on our sin so that we might have peace and be healed. If we look at the Hebrew version of this text, we find that, he took on our sins so that we might have *"shalom"* (peace), which means safety, health, prosperity and be *"raphah"* (healed), which means to be made thoroughly whole. God does not want us to lack anything in this life, including a healthy self-esteem. Jesus came to set us free. It is a gift, if we will receive it. Think about it, if Jesus came to set you free and to ensure your health and welfare, why would you ever have to walk with a hung-down head? My pastor, Bishop T.D. Jakes, has said, "The price of a product reflects its worth." God allowed his only begotten Son, Jesus, to die a horrible death on our behalf. Jesus was mocked, spat upon, and slapped by 500 soldiers. He had a crown of thorns pushed into his head and he received forty stripes with a whip, which ripped his flesh in every lashing. His hands and feet were nailed to the cross, his side was riven, and he poured out every drop of his blood for us. Will you look at the price God has paid for *you*? This price reflects the great worth God believes *you* have. We each have great worth in the sight of God. We are the righteousness of God in Christ Jesus. (See Rom. 3:22). Never forget this. Your embracing this is the key to your victory.

God loved us so much that he allowed Jesus to die in this manner. Jesus loved us so much that he willingly took our place and endured this death for us. We should appreciate his sacrifice by carrying ourselves like the women God created us to be. Smart women walk erect, with their shoulders square and their heads held high. We do not carry ourselves in a conceited fashion, but in a loving and totally confident fashion. How could we not walk in total confidence after being bought with such a tremendous price? It is time we begin to see ourselves as God sees us. When God the Father looks upon us, he sees us through the eyes of Jesus. When he looks at us through the eyes of Jesus, he sees us covered in the shed blood of Jesus Christ. He sees us forgiven of our sins and made brand-new because of the blood. He sees us as new creatures with old things passed away and all things having become new. (See II Cor. 5:17). He also looks upon us and sees himself because he, through his spirit, has come to dwell in us. With God living on the inside of us, we are *utterly priceless*. Armed with this knowledge, we never have to entertain the notion of walking in low self-esteem again.

I personally ceased from the "troublings" of low self-esteem several years ago. While vacationing during my early twenties, I met a lady who, by the world's standards, was extremely unattractive. She looked as though someone had run into her with a Mack truck and left her for dead. However, before I could feel sorry for her, I noticed that she carried herself as though someone had forgotten to tell her how she looked. "How could she look like this, but act like that?" I wondered. She, indeed, carried herself like one of God's women. She walked in a tremendous peace. She had her hair done in a nice style, which was very popular at the time, and she wore clothes which complimented her figure type. She was no small woman; however, she did not try to force a size 18 into an 8. She found stylish clothes which made her look wonderful. I found this woman intriguing. I could not fathom this peace she had. Suddenly, I found myself wanting to be like her. I wanted to have what she had. I wanted to be able to carry myself as she did, regardless as to whether the crowd accepted me. I vowed right then that I would never think of myself as "less than," due to flaws in my physical appearance. If God made me with an extremely large forehead and a flat chest, then so be it. I must have needed these things and not their opposite. I figured if this woman could walk around like a queen while looking as if she had been left for dead, then I could accept the things about me that I believed hindered my attractiveness. I began to remind myself how I am wonderfully made and how because of Jesus Christ, "I got it going on!" You have got it going on, too! The revelation I received from being around this lady and my subsequent study of Isaiah 53:4-5, caused me to let go of low self-esteem.

If you have not already, you certainly can let low self-esteem go, also. You are a woman of God and we are living in an age where we can be completely free of anything seeking to bind us. In this Spiritual Age, receive all that God has for you. Let Jesus teach you self-esteem. If you have not already, ask him to come into your heart and you will experience his love. Just pray simply,

"Father, I have sinned and fallen short of your glory. I believe that your Son, Jesus, has died for my sins and that you raised him from the dead. Thank you for this, Father. Now, Jesus I invite you to come into my heart, take away my sin, and be Lord over my life. I believe according to Romans 10:9-10, that I am saved. Thank you for saving me. Amen."

Bio

Min. Patricia D. Samuels, MA has been speaking in public (in churches and in schools) since the tender age of 10 and sought after for advice since even before then. While barely a woman herself, she was called upon to serve as the Women's Sunday School Teacher of the Salem Missionary Baptist Church of Port Arthur, Texas. In this position she was the youngest person in her class while serving students, some of whom were fifty years her senior. After receiving the Holy Spirit's Baptism, she began sensing the call to ministry, which many others had already seen in her, but which she denied. She reluctantly accepted her call, but "told" God that she would teach Vacation Bible School and an occasional Sunday School class in her "spare time" of jet-setting abroad as an International Corporate Attorney. God found this plan to be quite humorous. While teaching the Women's Sunday School class and accepting her call, she was again called upon – this time to teach the Sunday School lessons on the radio – to prepare listeners for their upcoming Sunday School classes. From this emerged the *"Walking Through The Scriptures With Patricia"* radio broadcast, hosted by her father, the late-great Bro. Jessie Samuels, Sr. - Gospel Promoter and Disc Jockey for over 50 years. In 2000, Patricia Samuels Ministries was incorporated to allow givers the opportunity to be blessed (through tax deductions) and in 2003 the ministry-intensive website, patriciasamuels.org, was launched. Additionally, Patricia obtained a Master's degree in Human Sciences (Psychology/Sociology) with the specific purpose of using it for Kingdom building. One Kingdom-building initiative is the International Association of Proverbs 31 Women [IAP31W], designed to empower Christian women from all over the world to successfully live the Proverbs 31 lifestyle! The ministry continues to grow; the Minister continues to grow.

In childhood and as a young adult, Patricia encountered many near-death experiences and was miraculously kept alive on several occasions. She was rescued from a burning house when she was an infant, kept from nearly severing a main artery at age 5, survived a train wreck at age 17, and survived an 18-wheeler collision at age 24. In retrospect, Satan's assassination attempts made the ministry call make sense.

Patricia has a special call on her life to encourage and exhort others to live victoriously based upon the principles of God's Word. Patricia's style of speaking is to-the-point, yet sensitive, sometimes humorous and always uplifting. Patricia believes that the ability to live the overcoming, victorious life is available to all who will receive it.

Patricia is a member of The Potter's House Church of Dallas, Texas where Bishop T.D. Jakes serves as Senior Pastor. At The Potter's House, Patricia sang for over eight years with the Grammy Award-winning Potter's House Mass Choir. Patricia is also a graduate of Texas A&M University; a member of Delta Sigma Theta Sorority, Inc.; and a member of the National Society Daughters of the American Revolution (DAR). Patricia is a testament that God is still in the blessing business.

Chapter 33

Waking Up

By Lori Anne Rising

I'm already dead. It's just a matter of time before my body follows.

The words slipped between my thoughts, startling me. I looked in the mirror. I knew I'd been stressed. I knew I had been eating less and less. In fact, I'd been feeling a lot of pride in my ability to stay in control and handle everything that happened that summer. I was not overeating as I had always done before to comfort myself, so I assumed I was doing well.

Wrong.

Staring back at me were gaunt, sunken holes for eyes; stringy, thinning strands that had once been thick, healthy hair; bony hips that just a month or so before had still been plump with left over baby weight. It occurred to me I had missed my period but I wasn't pregnant. No. I was in trouble.

I thought about giving up, but staring at my own mortality shook me to my core. Fear dropped down through me into a place I had never felt before; a place deep within me, but not inside me. It felt like an earthquake rattling my very soul. From the center of that quaking, I heard a voice rise up. A loud, resounding, terrified, *NO* echoed through me. Cleary, I was not ready to die, not yet. I had not done what I came to do. I had not even gotten started.

As I stood in the bathroom, listening to the hum of the fan, watching the rest of the steam evaporate from the mirror, I started thinking about my kids. My son was three; my daughter was still an infant. What kind of life was I modeling for them? I thought about my mother, fighting for her life all summer, having regret as her only form of stability. Is that what I wanted my life to become?

The awareness that I could walk out my door any time and not return, settled into my gut. I wondered, *if something happened to me today, would I be proud of the life I have lived so far?* I heard the woman in me, now calm, utter a soft but firm *No* and I felt the truth of it wash over me.

It had been a nightmarish summer.

In 2003, I was 27 years old. It was 6:30 am Tuesday morning in early June when my mother called asking for a ride to the hospital. I could not leave my 12 day old daughter so my husband went.

When he returned, he said she had a horrible headache and was nauseous but thought it was just the flu. He said she would call when she was ready for a ride home.

The phone rang only half an hour later but it wasn't my mom. I was alone in the bedroom when the nurse told me, "We did an MRI and found blood in her brain. We know it's a ruptured aneurysm but we don't have the facilities here to deal with it. We've already put her in an ambulance to Emanuel. They have specialists there. Her belongings are with her."

My mother had a birthday in less than a month. She was 49 and all I could think was, *my mother is dying.*

The bright morning sun dimmed as my sight narrowed and darkened; I thought I was going to pass out and would have welcomed the blackness.

I heard the words whispered in my ear, *she's coming home.* I felt the breath of a man's voice on my cheek. It was cool and calming. Instantly, every fiber of my being was filled with peace.

I was still alone in the room, staring out the window at the June day just beginning but she was going to be OK. I felt it. I *knew* it.

Until my mom's aneurysm, I had been taught to put everyone needs and happiness before my own.

From the outside looking in, I had a great job and a loving, growing family. I had achieved something very few in my family had earned... a bachelor's degree. We had a nice home in a good neighborhood, a couple of cars in the driveway and a great future.

It was not all perfect but I felt like I was on the "right" track, doing everything I had been taught I "should" do. I had utterly bought into the idea that if I took care of everyone else well enough and long enough, I would be taken care of too.

Wrong. And now, looking in the mirror months later, I realized I was paying for it.

Over these months, I had taken everything on. First, it was paying my mother's bills and feeding her cats, "just until she came home." Then, it was handling her divorce proceedings, "just until she came home." Then, it was handling the summer real estate business for my mother-in-law and partner, when she injured herself. After all, it was my job, my duty, to take it all on and take care of everything. It's what I had been hired for in the real estate business. And it's what a "good" daughter does... right?

Because I was so busy I decided it was best to skip breakfast because I needed to get to the office and the chaos of getting kids ready did not allow me time to eat.

When my daughter was about a month old, I decided to wean her off my milk. I knew my stress would impact her health if I continued to breast feed so, against the wishes of my husband, I disconnected myself from her. I realized too late that feeding her had been the one thing that reminded me to eat.

Once she was weaned, I went from just skipping breakfast to forgetting lunch until about mid afternoon. I didn't want to ruin my appetite for dinner, so I'd simply hold off another hour or two, suppressing the gnawing in my stomach with caffeinated tea and soda. I prided myself on the control I had and kept charging forward, handling multiple attorneys for my mom's affairs, dealing with 10 to 15 real estate transactions and playing mom, wife, and the good daughter as best I could.

As I began to lose weight, I heard comments about how good I was looking, so I figured I must have been doing something right. Besides, once the initial crisis was over, life would return to normal. My mom was coming home. That voice had told me so.

Then came the days when I came home completely exhausted. My stomach, all tied up in knots, refused to eat anything more than a few bites. I had gotten really good at hiding that fact that I was no longer eating regularly. If I tried, I would choke.

Staring at what I had become because of these choices, I began to question my life assumptions. That voice had said my mom was coming home, he had not said when and he did not say which "home".

I naturally assumed he had been referring to the one on this physical plane and it sounded like it would only be a few short months.

It had now been almost six months since her aneurysm. My mom's life was no longer on the line but she would never be the same and her affairs still needed my attention. Clearly, this was not ending anytime soon and I was killing myself trying to be everything I believed others wanted and needed me to be. I wanted to be proud of the life I was living now, today – and every day.

I began to think about what it might take for me to say "yes"; to feeling good about my life, maybe even for the first time. What would it mean to take care of myself? If I did, could I pursue my own dreams?

Wait. What dreams?

I could recall a time in my life as a child when I dreamt about what I would be when I grew up but in that moment, that morning, my dreams were so distant and disconnected from what I had become that I could no longer recall what they'd once been.

So I made a commitment to myself: I would take at least one step each day for the rest of my life until I could say, "Yes!" to pursuing my dreams.

It was not about whether or not I had completed what I set out to do, nor whether or not it turned out the way I planned but rather, "Did I do my part?" Did I take the steps I knew I could and needed to or did I put them off out of fear and fall prey to "shoulds" again?

As I walked out of the bathroom that morning, my thoughts began to spin in a new direction:

- What does it mean to live without "shoulds"?

- How will I know the difference between the "shoulds" and what's really *right* for me?

- Is there some part of me that exists without them; without the shoulds of my family, without the shoulds of my community, without the shoulds of my culture, or even of the time and place I was born into?

- What if there was?

- What if there was a part of me that just *is*; that *was* before this life and will *be* long after it?

- What if I could connect to *that* part of me in a way that could guide me? What if I could create a list of criteria from *that* place that I could bounce any choice off of and know that if it fit, it was me, and if it didn't, it wasn't?

- What if I could *live* from that place?

- What if the whole world could live from *that place*?

I wish I could tell you that life turned on a dime and everything was magically fixed somehow as I began to move forward but it wasn't. It would take a full year for my mom's affairs to be settled. It would take another three years before I could look back at that time and feel as if I was finally past it. This much I did know, that time changed me.

I can look back now and know that the voice that June morning had told me exactly what I needed to hear to allow the rest to unfold. I know I needed to change. And, I know from my journals that I had been calling out for that change long before my mom ever went into the hospital. I had unknowingly fought the process though, making the change hard and painful.

The awful realization was that all of this was my own doing but I know, absolutely, with every fiber of my being, that I would do it all again in order to be who I am today.

There were days in the beginning when my one step towards my dreams was nothing more than getting out of bed. Eventually, I took more steps and one day I fulfilled my first childhood dream: I wrote a book, becoming an author for the first time.

Over the years, I have also divorced, changed careers, and continued to pursue other dreams. It has not been easy, but it's been good because I learned to live from *that* place.

Today, I am still in process; always learning, always growing. Always fine-tuning how I want to express who and what I really am in the world. The "shoulds" still make their presence known but I have stopped living by them. Instead, when I look in the mirror at night and wonder, *"am I be proud of the life I lived today,"* I feel the subtle stirrings of joy as the woman in me rises up, whispering through my heart and mind, Yes. Yes. Yes.

Bio

Lori Anne is Certified Life Coach, author's coach and editor who helps speakers, thought leaders and experts from around the world write books that inspire hearts and minds. So far she's worked with authors in the U.S., Israel, Canada, Spain, Belgium, England, and Jamaica to help them share their stories, knowledge and wisdom while building their business.

She began her college years in psychology and criminology, with the intention of going into criminal profiling. She graduated with a BA in English and Women's Studies, and then went into real estate. She spent the first part of her adult life living for others, doing everything she believed she "should" do. Her mother's aneurysm brought her face to face with her own mortality, when she finally decided to reclaim her life.

She pursued life coaching in 2005 and published her first book, *Who Am I?*, in 2008. She worked with Compass Life Coaching in 2009 to co-create the Monthly Action Plan™ titled, *Rediscover Yourself*, based on her book. She has also published in Business Heroine Magazine, and been an expert author for SelfGrowth.com.

In 2010 she returned to school. As a Masters student in Leadership and Communications at Marylhurst University, Lori Anne is currently researching the top most influential nonfiction books to understand why they had the impact they have, so that she can teach the how to her clients. She expects to graduate in June of 2013, and publish her findings later in the year.

As a mom, she loves spending time with her two kids in the great outdoors of the Pacific Northwest, creating memories as often as possible. In her spare time, she enjoys cross stitch, hiking, painting, and the company of great friends.

To learn more, or follow her research, visit www.AuthorshipFor-Experts.com, or be a part of the conversation online at Facebook.com/AuthorshipForExperts

CPSIA information can be obtained at www.ICGtesting.com
Printed in the USA
BVOW071704030713

324938BV00001B/41/P